THROUGH ANIMALS' EYES, AGAIN

Stories of Wildlife Rescue

by

Lynn Marie Cuny

University of North Texas Press
Denton, Texas

10 9 8 7 6 5 4 3 2 1

Permissions:
University of North Texas Press
P.O. Box 311336
Denton, TX 76203–1336

The paper used in this book meets the minimum requirements of the American National Standard for Permanence of Paper for Printed Library Materials, z39.48.1984. Binding materials have been chosen for durability.

Library of Congress Cataloging-in-Publication Data

Cuny, Lynn Marie, 1951–
    Through animals' eyes, again : stories of wildlife rescue / by Lynn Marie Cuny.
        p. cm.

    ISBN-13: 978–1–57441–216–1 (cloth : alk. paper)
    ISBN-10: 1–57441–216–7 (cloth : alk. paper)
    ISBN-13: 978–1–57441–217–8 (pbk. : alk. paper)
    ISBN-10: 1–57441–217–5 (pbk. : alk. paper)

    1. Wildlife rescue—Texas—Anecdotes. 2. Wildlife rehabilitation—Texas—Anecdotes. 3. Wildlife Rescue & Rehabilitation, Inc.—Anecdotes. I. Title.

QL83.2.C852 2006
636.08'3209764—dc22

                                                      2006007394

Unless otherwise noted, photos are by Barbara Synodinos or Tim Ajax.

The author would like to thank the Summerlee Foundation for their generous support of the publication of this book.

Layout and design by Andy Kerr
Eisenbrauns Prepress Services
http://www.eisenbrauns.com/prepress

Contents

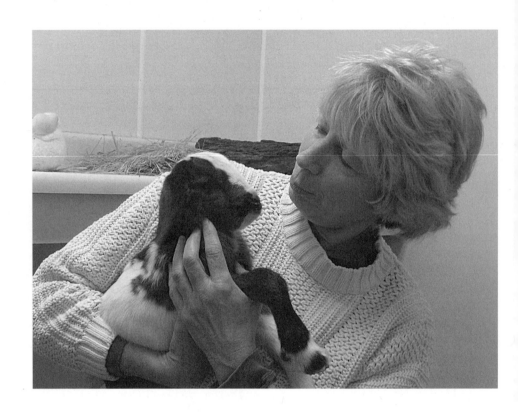

Preface

The book you are holding in your hands was never really intended to be a book at all. Since 1977 when I founded Wildlife Rescue & Rehabilitation, Inc., I have been writing the stories you will find in these pages for our Members Newsletter. Every day, as a primary aspect of my work, I am in the rare position to directly or indirectly encounter members of the non-human wild and domestic animal community. These were not always happy encounters. This is to be expected in the case of wild animals in particular, as they understandably have a natural fear and disdain for humans. However, they were, I believe, important encounters and only after literally years of being coaxed to do so, I have completed two books that are a compilation of stories of these meaningful "meetings" with animals.

I believe the most important function of these stories is that they approach the world of non-human animals from a perspective of deep respect and appreciation. You will not find in the pages of this book any tales of how wonderful it is to have a "pet" raccoon or monkey; you will not read about the bond between wild animals and humans. What you will find are true stories of the animal-to-animal bonds, relationships, rescues, and devotion. There are also stories about domesticated animals and what their lives, like that of their wild counterparts, are like in a world dominated by you and me. I have done my best to write what I feel might be taking place in the hearts and minds of the animals I have been fortunate enough to be of service to. I do not believe for a minute that we can ever really know their minds so I can only write what I have perceived through my flawed human screen.

If you have had enough of the animal horror stories, you will enjoy what I have offered in this manuscript. If you have ever struggled with the age-old questions, "do animals have feelings, do they think, share, want, mourn," you will find these stories enlightening. If you have had the good fortune of spending time as an unobtrusive observer of the other species who inhabit this earth then I think you will find this book most enjoyable. I hope that no matter what your interest in wild and domesticated animals might be, that you are touched by these stories recounting the lives of the animals who have made a profound difference in my life and the lives of all the people who have been a part of Wildlife Rescue & Rehabilitation, Inc. for these 30 years. It is my hope that *Through Animals' Eyes, Again* will move its readers to see animals in a new and more realistic light and that with that new vision we will all become more compassionate human beings.

The Lady Hawk

Have you ever been driving or sitting and reading or just going about your daily chores when something you see or smell or hear enlivens the memory of a particularly sweet and meaningful event in your life? This very thing happened to me when my partner, Craig Brestrup, and I were driving into San Antonio. As we drove through the remaining wooded areas along 281 North we passed a giant golf ball towering over the trees advertising a totally out-of-place golf course. I have seen this gaudy edifice countless times but for some reason this time I was reminded of the area that is situated well beyond that turn in the road.

When I was growing up in San Antonio in the 1950s, my parents purchased a small lot in a new "development" called Cypress Cove. I was the youngest of six and had the good fortune to be blessed with parents who were two of the finest people I have ever known. My mother and father loved nature and had a dream to one day, after all of us kids were raised and on our own, build a small house on that lot in Cypress Cove and spend their retirement years in the peace and quiet of the Hill Country. There was little or no peace and quiet for them while they were raising my five siblings and me, and they so loved the outdoors that this seemed a very fitting way to live out the last years of their lives. In preparation for the realization of their dream, they used to take me and a brother or two out to their favored spot so that we could all enjoy a day away from the city. And we kids would go there on our own to swim in the ponds and run off some of our endless energy. Thanks to our parents' influence we all loved nature and were happiest when we were climbing trees or sitting by a creek. It was not by accident that the Cuny home was the place to go if you lived in our neighborhood and had found a homeless dog or cat or if you encountered an injured or baby opossum, lizard, frog, or on one occasion, a red-tailed hawk.

One day, one of my brothers came home proudly toting a huge cardboard box. My mother always knew this meant there would be another mouth to feed—not a human mouth, but a mouth just the same. Though I cannot remember the details, I will always remember that inside that box was the most beautiful bird my young eyes had ever seen. The hawk had a badly, though not broken, injured wing and she was thin and almost lifeless. Most of what we did in those days to aid animals in need of help was probably a combination of some knowledge, a lot of guessing, and my mom's prayers along with all of our best intentions. We placed the huge bird in a large cage in our backyard. Though most folks did not have cages in their back-yard, there was always a big cage or two at the Cuny home. We immediately set about the task of trying to find something we hoped we could to entice her to eat. I remember that anything as expensive as a steak in those days would rarely make it into our house, but somehow for the hawk my mother managed to scrape together the funds to buy this beauty just what she needed to survive.

My brothers had fashioned a crude cast for her wing, and using a small pair of pliers they had to force the unwelcome food down her throat. Every day there was the ritual of trying to coax her to eat on her own and every day she would refuse. The poor, injured bird was terrified and wanted nothing but to be free again. I will never forget the spring morning that I went out to check on her with my mom and there in the cage sat a single, perfect egg. From that moment on my mom referred to our patient as "Lady Hawk."

Day after day, I would sit by the cage and peer inside at the ner-vous, disabled bird, as my mother would offer her soothing voice in an attempt to calm the nervous captive. I wondered where she came from and if she had left a family behind. I felt so sorry for her and so helpless to do anything to relieve her suffering. As a young girl, there was a part of me that wanted her to be calm and glad to see me but because my parents had taught us that wild creatures should be respected for who they are, I wished she could fly away. I think my mother felt particularly sad for this foundling. I remember she and my father talking about how unfair it was that someone so beautiful and wild should be crippled and possibly lose her ability to fly. Most of the animals brought to our home or found by one of us children were sturdy young opossums or horned lizards who always survived our care and curiosity. But to see this magnificent creature of the wild grounded and stuck in a cage in our backyard touched us in ways we had never before felt. My mother would not let a day go by without taking repeated breaks from her daily washing, ironing, and cooking to go out and do her best to reassure the bird she called, "Lady Hawk." I felt certain that some form of trust or even fondness was growing between these two. My mother was one of the most maternal and nurturing women I have ever known, and I believe that gentleness was not lost on the fragile hawk.

Finally after weeks of confinement and care, Lady Hawk was well enough to be set free. We were all a little amazed and thrilled that she had survived. When we talked about the best place for her to reclaim her freedom, there was little to discuss. Mom and Dad knew that she would be safe at Cypress Cove. As I recall, the privilege of releasing her went to my brother who had found her. Though none of us went along, we were given a full report of how, when the box was gently placed on the ground and opened wide to set her free, the bird who had once hovered near death, tilted her head to the sky, opened her bronze colored wings and in one flawless motion lifted her now strong body up into the air. Leaving the box and my brother behind on the leaf-strewn ground, she flew into the dense cover of the live oaks and after a quick survey of her surroundings took to the pure blue sky and flew out of sight. We were all happy that the release was a success, but I think my mom was more pleased than any of us. For months afterwards we talked about the big, beautiful bird who had touched our lives and was now somewhere in the Hill Country flying free. I think we were a little sad to know that we would never see her again.

It was the following autumn when one of my brothers and I went with our parents to spend the day at Cypress Cove. The air was crisp with an early cool front and the four of us walked along the edge of the creek talking as the dried, fallen leaves crunched beneath our feet. We were laughing and glad to be out-of-doors when, in only an instant, the calm of our surroundings was interrupted by the appearance of a large bird flying down the center of the creek. We looked up just as she landed on top of one of the oaks. Our conversations ceased and in that moment of total silence I heard my mother's soothing voice: "Lady Hawk, is that you?" The bronze beauty flew down even closer; now she was perched just above my mother's head. Again my mom's voice reached out to her: "How good to see you,

Lady Hawk." The now healthy bird tilted her regal head and looked down at my mom. She had heard my mother's voice as we walked along that day and something compelled her to come closer. The two ladies stood there remembering the time when they had met under very different circumstances. That time had been a sad one indeed, but today all that passed between them was a mutual remembrance, a greeting and an understanding that these two had shared something no one else would understand. The bird my mother called Lady Hawk sat for a few moments more; the two visited and then said their good-byes. As we reluctantly continued our walk, Lady Hawk flew down the center of the creek one last time, and as if to let my mom know that she was indeed well, shot up into the bright blue autumn sky and disappeared from our sight. We never saw her again, but when we would visit Cypress Cove and walk along that creek, we were serenaded by the not too distant call of a red-tailed hawk. My mother would always say, "There is Lady Hawk," and my father and I would smile and know she was right.

An Unusual Adoption

It is hard to believe that autumn is approaching because the calendar says August, but as I look out on the sanctuary grounds I see the shadows lengthen and each evening the stars appear just a bit sooner than the night before. Oddly enough, we are the happy beneficiaries of an unseasonable cool front, one more element that contributes to the overall autumnal mood of the last month of summer.

It was an August much like this one nine or more years ago when Wildlife Rescue was called to rescue a tiny, orphaned cacomistle. This is the beautiful slate gray and white nocturnal mammal so many folks refer to as a ring-tailed cat. The fact of the matter is they are not in the feline family at all; they are more closely related to their cousin, the ever-popular raccoon. It is this relationship that could help explain exactly why the unusual events unfolded as they did.

The baby cacomistle had lost her mother and her siblings to dogs who discovered the family nesting in the hollow of a huge, ancient hackberry tree. The mother had done her best to distract the curious and ultimately destructive dogs away from her young, but the dogs were persistent, large, and aggressive and the nocturnal family of this delicate species was none of those things. When the bloody site was discovered the following morning there was no one alive except for the, I suspect, "runt of the litter"—a little female who was now in our care. It was ironic because, not only was she small, but this remaining survivor was frail and probably would not have survived the rigors of growing up in the wild. But this is something we will never know—for now her family was dead and she was in our hands. And as is the norm, it was the time of year when our hands were very full.

There were squirrels, nestling doves, cardinals, and finches; there were raccoons and skunks but not one single cacomistle could be found except for this lone little girl. The moment she arrived we knew we had our work cut out for us because she was covered in blood, though her wounds were only scrapes and small cuts. It appeared that her mother had tried to move her. Perhaps it was her dying attempt to save her baby that had left this young one covered with her mother's blood. She was frightened and cold and wanting only the warmth of her family. We had no family to offer her; all we had were our honest attempts to keep her alive and enable her to grow into a strong juvenile and one day return to the wild.

But there were many events that were yet to occur before we would see the dawning of that day. In order to help her feel more at home and less alone in this foreign world, we placed the tiny female next to a litter of healthy, fat, rarely quiet, orphaned raccoons. They were only slightly larger and considerably more vocal, so much so that at times I wondered if the baby cacomistle would have preferred isolation to these raucous neighbors. But as the weeks passed and all the babies grew, she seemed to look and listen to her nearby relatives for comfort. Cacomistles have the sweetest of calls and when a baby is in distress and you hear this shrill alarm you want only to comfort the little one. But this little girl found better ways to find the emotional comfort she needed. The litter of raccoon babies growing up next door began to listen to their neighbor and when she would cry they would do the same; oddly it seemed to calm the infant cacomistle, though it set off a seemingly unending current of raccoon cries. The lone little girl would become quiet and take one of her regular naps as her neighbors railed on. This ritual repeated itself with reliable regularity until one day the lives of her neighbors were drastically altered.

It is our hope every time we rescue babies who have lost their mother that a surrogate will come our way to help care for and teach the youngsters. This only rarely occurs, but when it does it is the best thing that can happen to orphaned wildlife. One day we were met with the great good fortune (although terribly sad for other reasons) of just such a mother finding her way to our door. She was a young raccoon who had been hit by a car and if that was not bad enough, she had been caring for her own babies when the accident occurred. The people who hit her thought they were doing the right thing by keeping her in a cage in their backyard for two weeks after the accident. When her condition worsened they brought her to Wildlife Rescue. Upon examination it was clear that she had left behind a litter of young and sadly they too had most likely perished by now. The young mother was emaciated and had a badly infected rear leg.

She was also exhausted from trying her best to escape from her captors for two weeks, doing her best no doubt to get back to her babies. But now her babies were gone and she was in yet another frightening captive situation.

After several days of fluid and nutritional therapy, her condition improved. And being the ever-hopeful people that we are, we placed the new female in the same room as the young raccoons. There was no mistaking who this newcomer was in their quick, young minds. There was a mother in their midst and they knew it! The new mom, however, was not quite as enthused as the babies. She peered into their carrier and offered nothing friendlier than a quick, low growl. This immediately quieted the little ones and in no time an understanding was born. It was another week before she would behave in a caring fashion towards her new adoptees, but once she decided to take on the motherless youngsters, it was if they had been her very own from the very beginning. The day we knew they could officially call her "mother" began with an "accident."

After cleaning the female's cage, a volunteer failed to secure the latch on the door. In no time the mother raccoon left the confines of her cage and made her way to the large box holding the baby raccoons. She must have made several attempts to get in because the scratch marks on the side of the box were deep and the cardboard was severely shredded. But one attempt or twenty, by the time we came back into the room equipped with the formula for the youngsters and ready with our bottles and plans to feed them, they had already sat down to dinner. There in the bottom of that huge box that had once held a big-screen TV, was the most welcome sight we could hope to see. The once aching, babyless mother had found the litter of youngsters who had lost their own mother and in their own way, with no help from us, except the mistake of an open door, they had created a new family. There were all the sweet sounds of contented babies, sucking and cooing on their mom and her returning the love with her licks and upturned stomach. Our work for these beauties was done. Now all we had to do was to find the perfect safe site and set them free to begin again their life in the wild.

But out of this union came one tragedy. Now there would be no more baby coon sounds for the cacomistle. She still had no mother and now she did not even have the comfort from the sounds of those noisy neighbors. But nature has ways of taking care of her youngsters and this time would prove to be no exception. It was very late one night, all the babies had been fed, the birds were quietly perched in their areas and no one was stirring. No one except a small gray, furry, little female cacomistle who decided this was the night to go exploring. In all her weeks with us, she had remained safe in her large wire cage. There were limbs and leafy branches, a small dark area where she could hide and soft warm flannel bedding for all those midday naps. But tonight something stirred her spirit, something told her to move those tiny, scarred legs and go exploring for something better than a wire cage. I do not know how long the little girl had been out; there were some boxes of tissues knocked over, and a small bowl of water left out for a mouse was tipped and spilled on the floor. But the sight that I will never forget was the one I saw when I opened the door to the nursery. There in that dim light of late night was the new mother raccoon; she too had decided to squeeze her way free. It seems there was a baby crying and it was her job to look into the matter. And now she had that very baby in her jaws; our eyes met and all I could think of was that the young female cacomistle was soon to lose her life. After all the trauma and all the crying it seemed such a shame that she would end her life this way, killed by a mother of another species not all that different from her own.

I could not move fast enough and neither could the raccoon. She had lost one litter of young at the hands of careless humans, and she was not about to let it happen again. With that slim, gray body of the orphan cousin in her masked jaws, she pushed her way through the opening that had allowed her release and in a moment she was back in her cage. But she did not take this new baby there to kill her; no, this baby too would become one of her own. She lay the frail little female in the middle of her litter and then with her stomach upturned she lay next to her and began licking and encouraging the baby to nurse. The tiny cacomistle needed little encouragement; in only seconds she had taken her place amongst the new family and here she would stay until she was weaned. The mother raccoon loved and cared for her as if she too were her very own. As the weeks passed and the babies grew we moved the unique family to a large outdoor cage and it was in this cage that the little female learned to climb and play with her cousins and was weaned and made ready for the wild. When we set them free, they went back to the wild as a family; I do not believe they remained so for very long, but the babies, even the different one, will always remember the caring mother who not only took them in but who went searching one night for a baby in distress and brought back a cousin they could all call their own.

One Lonely Goose

It is always a comfort to have the privilege of observing members of the non-human animal kingdom. So often we think of them as victims—helpless, voiceless, and incapable of creating situations that make their lives more enjoyable. Fortunately, this is not the case. Often, when given the opportunity, non-human animals make the very decisions that significantly alter their lives. A perfect example of this is three geese who now live at WRR. The first is a tall and lanky China goose who came to us after his mate died.

For several weeks, the residents of the community surrounding a small pond had watched as a regal male and female China goose swam with the other geese and ducks who inhabited the neighborhood. It was obvious when the female became ill. She would sit listlessly at the pond's edge, protected by her faithful mate. Her head hung limp, her breathing was labored and slow. But as soon as anyone would approach her, she would waddle into the safety of the water, followed dutifully by her mate. Though the residents knew she needed help, they were unable to catch the goose or offer her any relief. Several weeks passed and the female showed no improvement. She began to lose weight. The fresh bread and scratch feed offered to her were rejected. Often, the male would do his best to coax his mate to eat; he would probe about in the dish of corn and seed and look up to the female to see if she was interested. Day after day, she would just sit, show no interest, and grow weaker by the moment. Finally, just at sunset, one of the residents walked down to the pond to offer food to the dying goose. He watched in amazement as the female slowly waddled out into the water, the male close behind as always. As the female approached the center of the pond, she began to slowly sink deep into the water. The male goose made continued efforts to hold her up. He gently slipped his strong neck under her sinking body, but the female would not accept his help. She swam away into deeper water. As the male followed, all he could do was watch. He floated quietly behind her, trying to keep her alive, calling to her, but she had made her decision. Slowly and without a sound, the beautiful female goose sank below the water's surface.

The male called out to her again and again, but she was gone. Nothing he could do would bring her back. The lone male goose sat silently in the cold water. He called and waited and waited. Several ducks came near, three other geese swam to his side, but he just remained swimming in the very spot where the female had drowned. Two hours later he swam to the bank and took his place where he had always sat by his mate's side. The neighborhood residents brought him treats of dry dog food and wild birdseed. He would not eat. For four days this ritual of refusing help continued, the widower goose just sat on the banks in the dry grass. He would not go into the pond. He would not eat, only now and again would he call out to his missing mate. A week passed, still no change. WRR was called out to rescue the bereaved goose. He did not even run away when our volunteer approached. The male goose had given up his will to live.

When he arrived at the sanctuary, his behavior did not change. It was our hope that in the company of so many other geese, males and females, he would find some welcome companionship and, at best, even choose a new mate. But the Lone Goose did not mingle with the other China geese. He did not waddle to the pond; the very most he would do was eat the food we offered. But even this he did with little interest. Weeks passed and the goose quietly accepted his new home and his new surroundings. Once in a while, several of the other resident geese would come near, but then only to fight and try to drive the Lone Goose out of their area. He was not welcomed at the pond's edge; he was not welcomed at the community feeding bowls. His world had become one of solitude; he was literally surrounded by his own kind and yet he was totally alone. His only salvation was to come in the form of not one, but two more social rejects.

Weeks after Lone Goose came to live at the sanctuary, we rescued two more geese. These two, like Lone Goose, had nothing in common, socially speaking, with the resident geese. One of these birds was a beautiful pen-raised Canada goose, regal in his black, brown, and white plumage. He took his place on the pond, floating about, his dark head diving beneath the water's surface, coming up to call out in his native tongue to no one in particular. No other goose spoke his language, but he would call just the same. He seemed content enough, life as a single male did not seem to be a problem for him.

The second of these was a rare bird compared to the more "common" China and Embden geese living at the sanctuary. This new fellow was an Egyptian goose, a domestic breed loved for their smaller build, their unusual call, sounding very different from a typical goose "honk," and their colorful orange and brown head. This goose seemed to fit in better with the ducks; he would often be seen having his breakfast with them near the pond, and only on occasion would he frequent the "goose gatherings." But soon these complex social structures would experience a permanent change.

Every once in a while, a staff member would notice the lonely goose sitting under the stand of junipers near the nutrition center. There he would be in his pitiful state, just honking and looking out as dozens of geese passed by, ignoring him or stopping just long enough to try to pick a fight. But every so often, the regal Canada would waddle up under the junipers and squat down several feet away from him. He would not stay long, but the visit was definitely a friendly one. One sunny afternoon, the Egyptian goose decided to join the twosome who looked cool and comfortable in the shade of the juniper bushes. He, too, decided to make himself at home. Finally, there was a ray of hope for the lonely male goose.

Days passed and little changed with the threesome. Together they would sit in their favorite spot; food and water now placed nearby, just seeming to enjoy being together. It had been over a month and a half. Lone Goose was still his stoic self. Would he ever come out of mourning for his mate? Early one Wednesday we were to have our answer. The staff began the morning feeding ritual. The wild birds in the aviaries were the first to be fed. Then the trays of food were being prepared for the geese and ducks by the pond. As fresh seed, lettuce, and sliced vegetables were being loaded into the wheelbarrow just yards away from the goose threesome, something caught the interest of Lone Goose. Perhaps it was the food, maybe it was just that he had finally grown tired of waiting, but suddenly, like a bolt, he came waddling as fast as his big orange, webbed feet would carry him out from under the junipers. He was honking and calling out to the other geese and heading straight for the ankles of the staff member who was preparing everyone's breakfast. All of a sudden he was on a mission. He had been in mourning long enough. He had been sullen and alone as long as he could bear it. Now he was ready to resume his life as a goose, and just ahead were a pair of unsuspecting ankles.

The Canada and the Egyptian geese were as surprised as the staff member, but everyone seemed in agreement: if a pair of ankles was what was needed to revive Lone Goose, then so be it. With his two new companions close behind him, he stopped only inches away from the tasty ankles. His long, lanky neck was in perfect form for an attack goose, but his kind heart wouldn't let him do it. He proudly backed away, honked his threat of "maybe next time," and strode fearlessly down to the pond. But now he was not alone. Now no one came to challenge the once sad goose. Finally, two loyal friends surrounded him. Socially unacceptable though they were, to him they would become a new and perfect family. To this very day you can see Lone Goose, the regal Canada, and the Egyptian goose keeping constant company—just the three of them on the sanctuary grounds, the alternative to traditional goose family life and the perfect answer to a sad goose's lonely call.

Home Is Where My Sheep Is

Many times in its history, WRR has been called on to rescue animals who do not fall under the heading of "wildlife." Often, in the very early days, we were not usually able to take these animals in as we do today. Instead, we had to do our best to place them in good, caring, and permanent homes. Fortunately, in those days, many of the homes were provided by our members.

Early in the year of 1978, WRR was called on to rescue one very large, yellow and white tabby cat named Seymore. His person had just passed on and there were no family members who could take Seymore. About this same time, we were asked to find a home for an elderly Suffolk Sheep named Shefield. When these animals arrived at WRR, it was easy to see that both had been well-cared for and were not happy about having to leave their familiar surroundings. While working diligently to locate the perfect people for the two, Seymore and Shefield were kept together in a large outdoor enclosure. Seymore had a cozy cat house and Shefield preferred the green grass and his favorite spot under a small oak tree. Often you would find the two sleeping together. Seymore enjoyed curling up on Shefield's back and Shefield would often assist Seymore in finishing off his bowl of dry cat food. Every time a volunteer walked into the enclosure to play with Seymore, he was always followed by one large, wooly sheep.

In only three weeks, we had located the perfect home for Shefield. A small farm, about twenty acres, owned by one of our members. They were a middle-aged couple who loved animals. They had two small dogs, several ducks, geese, and two goats. When they arrived at WRR to take the sheep home, they noticed that he and Seymore had become good friends. The couple decided to take both of the "orphans" with the agreement that as soon as we found a home for Seymore, he would be sent there. In less than a week, the cat and the sheep had settled into their new home. They had become acquainted with the resident goats, ducks, and geese, but Seymore was not particularly fond of the two small dogs. He was bigger than the two put together, so perhaps he was not convinced that they were dogs at all. Shefield ignored the goats; they were close to being sheep but after all, he had Seymore, so hoofed friends were not required. Every morning when breakfast was delivered, Seymore and Shefield stood side by side, waiting patiently to share their favorites treats. Every night would find the two sleeping quietly, one yellow cat curled up comfortably on the back of a content, sleeping sheep. But soon, this friendship would meet its end.

Not long after Seymore and Shefield arrived at their new home, a call came in to WRR. A young woman had just moved to Texas, had purchased a house, and was in search of a cat to keep her and her elderly cat company. As soon as she visited Seymore, she fell in love with him and whisked him off to his new home. Now Shefield would have to learn how to be one of the farm animals. Suddenly, he was alone. There was no one to eat breakfast with except the goats. At night there was no one to curl up and sleep on his back. It did not take long for Shefield to let everyone on the farm know that he was not happy. He would not eat. He would spend his days and nights just moping under the small oak tree. Seymore was not faring much better. He was not compatible with his new roommate. He sulked in a corner of the room just under the windowsill. Every night he would walk about the house meowing in loud, sad tones. Five days passed, Cat and Sheep were both depressed. Seymore took it upon himself to do something about the intolerable situation. It was late one night, the moon was shining, the cat door was not latched, and one yellow and white tabby had a plan. He may not have known it at the time, but included in his plan was over twenty-seven miles of never-before-seen roads, fields, bridges, and one very well-traveled highway.

When Seymore was discovered missing, WRR was immediately contacted. His new person was certain that he would come out of hiding in a day or two, but two days passed and Seymore did not show. Everyone at WRR felt certain that he was on his way to She-field. We contacted the folks at the farm and they agreed to keep an eye open for the traveling cat. Over one week passed, there was no sign of Seymore; Shefield had decided to occasionally dine on some fresh, green alfalfa, but he was still sleeping away most of his days and every lonely night. Two weeks and still no Seymore. We were all beginning to worry. Twenty-seven miles was a long walk for anyone, especially a lone cat who was vulnerable to cars, dogs, and the ever-present threat of losing his way. It was about 11:00 p.m. when the storm hit with heavy rain, lightning, and gale force winds. We were all thinking the same thing: How would Seymore find his way in such a storm? The rain fell in sheets and the wind did not let up. Hours passed, now it was 4:00 a.m. and still no yellow and white tabby. Exhausted from waiting and worrying, the volunteers decided to get some sleep. The couple at the farm promised to call if there was any sign of the missing feline.

Early the next morning, though everything was covered in mud, the sun rose bright and warm. On the small farm, the dogs were barking, the ducks and geese were playing in the rainwater puddles, and the goats were anxious for their breakfast. But Shefield was not rising from under his small oak tree. He was sleeping later than usual. Perhaps the storm had kept him up all night. Or, maybe it was the large, yellow and white, dripping-wet lump that was so comfortably sleeping on his back that enticed him to sleep in on this beautiful morning. Without a doubt, Seymore the Traveling Cat was very grateful for the warm soft bed that his companion, Shefield, was so willing to provide.

When presented with his alfalfa breakfast, the thoughtful sheep lifted his head, looked over his shoulder at his very own cat, and politely refused. Seymore had risked his life, traveled for miles, survived an incredible storm, and made his way back to the sheep and the small farm that they could now, and for the rest of their days, call home.

Rookery Rescue

It seems that almost every day we learn that another green space has fallen under the blade. Even though we are disturbed as more trees are killed and more natural habitat destroyed, we watch from a safe distance as this occurs. For the wild animals living in these areas, the experience is quite different.

Late in the summer of 1999, the local newspapers, radio, and television news media reported an incident that took place in south San Antonio, Texas. There lay a quiet, wooded spot that for many years, hundreds of egrets called home. This home had everything the birds needed: tall, densely foliaged green trees, the nearby river, plenty of insects, and best of all, perfect nest sites. This quiet spot was so perfect that the egrets returned year after year to lay their eggs and rear their young. Sadly, all of that was soon to change.

It seems that an individual who either was not aware of the egrets' presence or was simply not sympathetic to the birds owned this perfect spot.

Spring and summer is the time when most wild animals have their babies. By mid- to late summer, these babies are ready to begin to take the steps that are critical to their survival. In the case of raccoons, skunks, squirrels, and deer, this means going out with mom to learn skills such as foraging, hunting, climbing, and swimming. In the case of birds, it means learning how to fly, forage, wade, and watch for predators. Sadly, there was one predator that even the most wary of birds could not avoid.

Early one morning in late August, the deafening roar of bulldozers shattered the peace and quiet of the egrets' world. Not one of us can even begin to imagine what it is like to be spending a quiet morning among the trees when suddenly, out of nowhere, your world begins to crumble all around you.

Only a few hours later, Wildlife Rescue's phone began ringing with frantic calls from nearby residents. The same story was repeated call after call: fledgling egrets, parent egrets, all were in grave danger and many were already dead. Trees were crashing to the ground, and in the trees, were dozens of nests where helpless young birds were calling out to their parents who, when possible, were escaping and flying overhead shrieking out warning cries to their young.

Susan Hughes and several other members of the Bexar Audubon Society were already on the scene and had contacted the U.S. Fish and Wildlife Service. Egrets are a protected species, but it was too late for some of the birds and many of the trees they had called home.

Wildlife Rescue agreed to take any birds who were unable to fly. In only a few days, we had received twenty-three injured and severely traumatized egrets. One by one, the birds were placed in quiet, dark carriers. One of the most life-threatening aspects of care for wild animals in captivity is the captivity itself. A dark and quiet environment was vital, especially to these poor birds who had been so severely traumatized.

We would soon learn that the damage done to these beautiful, snowy-white birds was in all too many cases fatal. Despite the best efforts of rescuers, five egrets died in route to the sanctuary. In only a matter of days, six more egrets died. Those who were hanging on were doing so against all odds. Time and time again, in one fragile body after another, we found shattered bones, fractured wings, broken legs, and mangled feathers. Bulldozers are not humane machines; they are as indiscriminant as every decision to destroy wildlife habitat.

Over the next several weeks, two more birds lost what had been their fragile hold on life. By late October, we were caring for the remaining ten birds. They were, with the exception of one still recovering from a leg injury, ready to make their way back into their world. Because the home of their parents and their parents before them had been destroyed, we had to find a new and safe site for their release.

On November 5, 1999, Wildlife Rescue's Tim Ajax and Susan Hughes arrived at Mitchell Lake in San Antonio. Once a wastewater treatment center, this area has for years been a haven to many species of migratory water and shorebirds as well as countless other species of beautiful migratory birds.

As their carrier doors were opened, the shy egrets, their broken bones healed, their fear momentarily put aside to survey their reclaimed freedom, took long, careful steps back into their world. One at a time, the first five birds emerged from the crates, extended their wings, and took to the cool, blue, autumn sky. Finally life could begin again. Soaring up to catch the November breezes, these courageous birds had survived the worst experience of their lives and now that experience was tucked away in the past, no longer able to harm them. The remaining reluctant four birds needed a bit more time and privacy to make their way back. But they too, from a quiet wooded spot, knew that it was time to go home. All nine egrets flew to freedom that day. It was sad indeed that more of their families did not survive. But because of those birds that are now back in the wild, there is hope for future generations of egrets to return to their new homes and begin again the tradition that was so violently taken from them.

The Egrets' New Home

The rains began late on a Saturday night. Here at Wildlife Rescue, we were initially grateful because finally it seemed that this parched, dry earth was going to feel some relief. For weeks we had been rescuing wild animals who were suffering because of the drought conditions in the area. By early Monday morning it was clear that this was to be something other than simply relief from a long dry spell. Heavy rains can be devastating to infant wildlife and floods are certain to take a tremendous toll on helpless babies of all species. The Wildlife Rescue telephones began ringing early Monday morning. The majority of calls were concerning baby birds who had fallen from the trees, often nest and all. In most cases, mother and father birds were nearby doing their best to care for their young in the midst of the pouring rain. By midday, the calls were also concerning white-tailed fawns; some were trapped by the swollen creeks, others were soaked and cold, crying for a mother who had been washed downriver. The news had to keep reporting on the now dozens of people in danger from the flood waters, but there was another community of beings who were also in dire need of help.

The wildlife in the flooded counties were battling to stay alive and to take care of their babies. The calls tripled by Tuesday afternoon. More fawns, now baby raccoons, opossums, snakes, squirrels, and even tiny, infant skunks were being washed up out of their dens. At the Boerne and Kendalia sanctuaries, we, too, had to deal with the rising water. In Boerne, enclosures were being inundated with rushing water that was carrying debris of every shape and size. In Kendalia, the earthen dams on our ponds were hit so hard that in a thunderous roar the dams burst and suddenly the Little Blanco River reclaimed her original route. The road to the Kendalia sanctuary became impassable. Staff could not get within miles of Wildlife Rescue. Fortunately the live-in interns were able to continue providing care for the animals. It was difficult for the Wildlife Rescue volunteers in San Antonio to get to all of the animals who needed their help. But somehow through perseverance and determination they kept doing their job. Some even managed to find a way through Blanco so that they could bring rescued animals to Kendalia.

In the midst of all of the chaos, we really did not expect a call from the San Antonio Zoo. But the native wildlife who live on and near the zoo property were having their problems too. WRR had been called on earlier to help the egrets who were left homeless after their rookery was bulldozed. Because the egrets' home was destroyed, the birds were forced to find a new home where they could safely raise their young this year. The egrets chose a group of large trees near an area called Big Lake at the zoo. When the rains came, some of these trees came crashing down into the water. According to zoo staff, there were egret nestlings, fledglings, and adults all clamoring to hold on to the broken branches and toppled foliage. For some reason, the zoo officials did not choose to provide care for these snowy-white birds. One staff member expressed concern that the egrets would not survive. Wildlife Rescue was called, and in less than two days, we were caring for ninety-eight homeless egrets.

The first group came late in the afternoon. There were several plastic tubs filled with rain-soaked, hungry, cold birds. Egrets have long, spindly legs. These are even more obvious on the nestlings whose bodies take up less space than those long, gangly legs. And this first clutch of babies seemed to be nothing but legs. But as soon as we were able to warm them and dry their feathers, their mouths became the more dominant part of their anatomy. These birds had been through a terrible time. Many of their family members did not survive the incident, they were frightened, and they needed and wanted some food. Nestling egrets, like most wading birds, have a unique and endearing appearance. They possess a rather scrawny looking body, pencil-thin, long legs, and a sturdy arrow-straight beak that begins where two bright, dark eyes stop in the midst of an explosion of spiked feathers. They have a voice that is deep and crackly. They are tenacious birds who learn at an early age that being precocious will probably save their lives.

I was fortunate to be in the clinic when the first rain-soaked band of baby egrets were brought in the door. I looked into the clear, plastic tub and in the midst of this heap of bird life sat the tiniest of babies. This little fellow looked as if he had just given up on life. I could only imagine what kind of a day he had experienced. We were dealing with pouring rain and hundreds of animals to feed, but he was dealing with holding on to life. There was something about this little one—he was so sad, he had lost his mother, his home, and now here he was in a strange place being picked up by a human—could things get any worse? One by one we quickly examined each bird. This group was fortunate, no broken legs or wings, just tired, cold, and hungry. We separated the birds into smaller groups, placed heat lamps over their makeshift nests, and as their food was prepared, we all wondered how many more animals would be coming through our doors that day.

The rains persisted, as did the flow of animals coming to the sanctuary: more fawns, raccoons, mockingbirds, skunks, ringtails, and even more egrets. By day four we were praying for the rain to stop. During every waking moment, everyone at Wildlife Rescue was doing all in their power to dry, feed, and keep the bodies and souls of incoming animals together. And through all of this activity there sat one tiniest of all baby egrets. His spirit had not recovered, but at least he was willing to take some of the nourishing food we offered. He was in a warm, wooden box with two other youngsters; there was no one as small as he was so we had to watch to be sure he was not trampled or pecked by his new family members. As the days passed, so did the rains, and we were up to our ankles in mud, but at least we could relax when we looked outside and saw an occasional patch of blue overhead. The road to the sanctuary was being repaired and staff was able to come and go. Life was not back to normal but it was at least more manageable.

Our tiniest of baby egrets was beginning to show some sign of recovery as well. I lifted him out of his nest box late one afternoon to offer him some food; at this age you usually have to open those pointed beaks and gently push the food toward the back of their mouth. But this little fellow was having none of that; he looked up at me with those piercing dark eyes, turned his beak toward the clump of meat, and in one swift movement, gobbled down a chunk the size of a small meatball. Our little guy was on his way. Perhaps he had decided that since he had survived all the other recent traumas life had presented him, that he could handle this one as well. Over the coming weeks I would have the great privilege of watching the hundreds of animals who were rescued during the storms grow strong and independent. We did not save every life that was brought to us, but we did save hundreds of them. Entire litters of raccoons, skunks, and opossums were rescued and have since been set free. Literally hundreds of wild birds who came to us looking like there was no hope for them are now flying free in the huge oak and hackberry trees here in Kendalia. And of the over 120 egrets who found their way to Wildlife Rescue more than two-thirds survived. For these milk-white, graceful, and fragile birds who have twice lost their homes, we can now offer them a new and *truly* safe home. A home here at the Wildlife Rescue sanctuary where we have already released dozens of the rescued birds. A home, I am happy to say, where they seem to be choosing to stay. For now every day you can look into the sky that hovers over the sanctuary and you will see flying there the most pure white, graceful, long-legged birds. And somewhere in the midst of the those beauties is one little fellow who not so very long ago was the tiniest of babies, cold and with little hope. He looked as if he had just given up on life; he had lost his mother and his home, but he had not lost the spirit that inspired him to keep trying, to hang on, and to survive the worst day of his life.

The Grand Old Girls

How many times in our lives are we faced with the opportunity, or perhaps a better word is challenge, of making what is decidedly a difficult decision? In the world of not-for-profit animal protection, these decisions usually consist of issues that deal with such things as: Which medication is the best for a particular illness? When is an animal ready to be set free? and Who will be able to adapt to a life in captivity? Then there are those decisions that make us step back and ask the question that goes to the heart of why we are here.

WRR learned from Craig Brestrup, Director of The Association of Sanctuaries, that there were twenty-three rhesus macaque monkeys in a lab in Michigan who were either going to be retired to a sanctuary or put to death. The day we received the call we were told that the monkeys had only two weeks to live and that we had to make our decision now. The image of twenty-three mostly elderly, female primates who had lived out their days isolated in small lab cages enduring heaven-knows-what and now facing imminent death was not an easy one to shut out. I knew we had nowhere to put them; I knew we were in the middle of organizing two major fund-raising events; and I knew we already had plenty of needy animals to care for. But the image of these old girls would not go away. It seemed to me it was time for one of those fortunately familiar leaps of faith. So I called the technician at the lab and told her we would make the commitment to taking the girls, but we would need a little more than two weeks to prepare. Being the primary person in the lab who was lobbying for the monkeys' release, she was thrilled. After faxing all the necessary paperwork to prove that Wildlife Rescue would provide a good home for the girls, we were accepted as the monkeys' new home.

Now the fun began. Planning not only how to, but also where to house the new residents was going to be a challenge. These girls had never been together in the lab, their lives had been made up of years of solitude—no touch except when they were being taken from their cages for an experiment, no time or opportunity to establish what is vital for non-human primates—solid relationships with other monkeys. So with the collective talent of WRR staff managers we devised a plan for relatively small, but temporary housing that would allow us to slowly introduce the girls and at the same time have them outdoors, unlike their over twenty years of life in a lab where they had been housed in a basement. The construction under way, it was now time to figure out how to transport the monkeys from Michigan to our sanctuary in Kendalia. We moved forward with the invaluable help of WRR's friends and volunteers: David Seelig who lives in Boston, Don Barnes from San Antonio, James Bias, Executive Director of The Bexar County Humane Society, and April Truitt of Primate Rescue Center in Kentucky. A transport van from The Humane Society was secured and made ready. WRR staff members Tim Ajax and Shemia Splonskowski drove to the humane society to pick up the van and equip it with the necessary transport cages. Intern Kathleen Riordan, accompanied by David Seelig, was ready when the day finally arrived for their cross-country journey that would end with the twenty-three monkeys here at their new home.

In only a matter of days, the twenty-three rhesus were here. It was late in the evening when they arrived, so they had to spend their first night in their transport carriers. But early the next morning, WRR staff was ready to move the new monkeys into their temporary home. It was obvious by their behavior that these girls had been isolated long enough. So instead of placing them alone and giving them time to get acquainted, we took the chance that they knew better than we did and placed the girls in three groups. None of us can begin to imagine what twenty plus years of solitary confinement are like. We cannot imagine being deprived of the touch of our own kind or what it is like to live most of your life deprived of a visit into the outside world of fresh air and warm sunshine. This is the life "lived" by millions of animals used in research every day. Until now, this was the life for these endearing female monkeys.

As they emerged from their carriers, some were cautious, and others darted out anxious to see what new sights surrounded them. But one emotion was common in each pair of curious, frightened eyes. Each female rhesus knew that her life was now quite different. Each old girl sensed that perhaps this was not a place to be afraid of, that a profound change had taken place, that something here was very different indeed. How long had it been since their acute sense of smell detected something other than an antiseptic kind of clean? How far back did their memories have to reach to recall the sound of birds singing in the trees? Did each of them instantly recognize the soft feel of a warm, summer wind as it caressed their faces that years before had felt the pain of the tattoo? As they looked around them, all the girls could see were oak trees and acres of green grass punctuated by rocks and bushes. Grasshoppers and cicadas chirped and called, axis deer meandered past, sniffed at the new monkeys, and moved on. Resident cows and sheep dropped by to see who was occupying the new enclosures. All of these new sights, sounds, animals, and sensations are now part of their world. But most important is the newness of having another monkey to touch, to groom, to sometimes chase and fuss with, to sit and sleep next to, to be comforted by, to reassure, to finally after years of solitude share a day and a night with.

What began as a reluctant decision to offer our help has now become a mission to create a truly perfect home for the new monkey girls. For now, the girls have their temporary enclosures, but as with all animals coming to WRR, so much more is necessary. We must build for these monkeys what we will be building for all the primates living at the sanctuary. Thanks to the donations we've received, a one acre enclosure surrounding an oak grove is in the monkey girls' future.

As they settle in, the female rhesus must know that the sanctuary is their final home. Non-human animals live in constant touch with their deepest sense of knowing. Now these amazing old girls who have been through so much, look out from their new dwellings and see only peaceful surroundings. Never again will an approaching human be a harbinger of fear, never again will they be tattooed or restrained; there will be no more days of darkness. From this moment forward their lives will be that of cherished, respected guests. They will be cared for and loved, they will be seen only as dear, gentle ones. No longer are they "tools." For finally they have been brought home; finally their work is done. Their suffering is over.

The Grand Old Girl Adopts a Daughter

We rarely have the privilege of getting to know a tiny baby wild animal, to watch her grow, and to finally see her once again in the company of her own kind, thriving and being loved and cared for close to the very way nature intended. But this past year I was just so privileged.

It was early summer when we received the call. An infant rhesus monkey had been a victim of the cruel trade in wildlife. She, like all helpless infants who are exploited by this business, had been ripped away from her mother's care shortly after birth to be sold into the "pet" market. These sensitive, intelligent animals are abused and exploited—all for the sake of profit to the breeders and dealers who continue to benefit by making innocent animals suffer. This particular baby had been purchased by someone who was no longer able to care for her. She had become "destructive" and had to be removed from their home. The fact of the matter was that she should never have been made available for purchase; wildlife belongs in the wild, not cooped up in living rooms or in backyards forced to live out their days in cruel confinement.

The baby monkey girl was scared when she arrived at the sanctuary. In her brief life she had lost her mother and now once again she was facing a strange and, to her, very frightening new world. She cried and clung tightly to her few stuffed animal friends. She would take her formula from her bottle and the warm milk seemed to comfort her, but there was no doubt that all she really wanted was her mother. We could love and care for her but we could not replace her mother—her mother who was, I am sure, crying for her lost baby girl.

The days passed and the infant seemed to realize that Wildlife Rescue was now her new home. We furnished her cage with soft, billowy hammocks fashioned from bed sheets; she had a mirror and teddy bears and dolls and all manner of things to do. As she settled in, and as some of her fear abated, we gave her the run of the room. She loved to spring off the top of the cage to the top of the curtain rods and slide down to the soft, carpeted floor. Once on the floor she would run as fast as she could, grabbing some of her favorite bedding as she ran, wrapping it around her entire body so that by the time she reached the other side of the room she was encased in bed sheets like a cocoon with long, furry legs. This wonderful game was enhanced when my little dog, Boris, was invited to play along with the monkey girl. The two would chase about the room, Monkey Girl on Boris's back holding on for dear life to the long, soft, blonde dog fur, just as she had once held fast to her mother's gentle coat. No doubt this eased some of her longing because the baby would often chirp and smile as only baby monkeys can. One of our staff tried to help by rescuing a kitten off of death row at animal control and bringing her as a friend for the little monkey girl. Though the infant monkey was too exuberant for the kitten (we named her Monkey Toy), the two did share the common bond of trying to adjust to life without their mothers. Monkey Toy now lives the life of a pampered and loved companion to a WRR volunteer and her family.

But the infant monkey had no family to go to. *We* had to serve as her family and we were woefully inadequate because we are not rhesus monkeys. Wild creatures belong with their own kind just as much as you and I do. But fortunately it would not be long before there would be a chance at a better life for this sad orphan. As the months passed, the monkey girl grew more comfortable with her surroundings and with the other animals here at the sanctuary. As she grew more independent, we were able to let her spend the warm summer days out of doors, under our watchful eyes, romping freely in the huge oak trees. She had her very own blue wading pool that sat under the cool, leafy canopy. Monkey Girl loved to climb to the low hanging branches of the oak tree, her tiny hands gripping the limbs as she adventurously hung as if on a bungee cord, only to drop without a care into the refreshing water below. Once immersed, she would swim along the shallow bottom in continuous circles amazing me at just how long she could hold her breath. She would surface only after every hair was completely soaked and then in one good, vigorous shake, she would splatter the ground with water and in only a moment Monkey Girl was a fluffy baby once again. This game of dive and swim was a favorite, second only to spending time in the pig pasture. If you have ever had the joy of getting to know a pig, you know that they are some of the most accepting of all animals. They are gentle and forbearing at times when many would be intolerant and unyielding. Monkey Girl would spend hours on the back of Fred, the largest of the pigs, holding tight to his large, hairy ears and even lying down to nap in the huge pile of her snoring, sleeping pig friends.

But soon after she found friends in the pig community, another more closely related friend arrived at Wildlife Rescue. There was an elderly rhesus monkey who was part of a larger group of monkey females that we rescued from a research lab in Michigan. She was having a difficult time fitting in with the monkey troop. This particular old girl is, I suspect, the oldest of them all; she is a tad overweight and round and soft, the perfect mother figure and temperament. And "mother" is exactly who she became here at Wildlife Rescue. After a few weeks of watching her, of noticing her innate gentleness, it was clear to staff member Tim Ajax that with her we had the chance of finding what the baby monkey most needed.

I will never forget the day I had to pull Monkey Girl away from her newfound pig family. Here she had found a community of friends; but in time she would grow and as she did she would need the company and like-minded life of her own kind. The sooner we forced her to make the break the better, and hopefully the easier it would be. She screamed and cried as I carried her down the sloping grassy area away from her pigs. It was all I could do to keep myself from turning around and taking her back. But what lay ahead, I was sure, would be better in the long run. We had moved the elderly monkey into the new enclosure. Here, I hoped, with all the room to run and climb in the treetops, the baby and the matriarch would have the perfect surroundings in which to get acquainted. I walked in with the youngster; in only moments she stopped crying and began to climb to the very tiptop of the oaks. She swung on the yielding branches and grabbed the tender leaves as a perfect midday treat. On the grassy floor of their new home sat one very wise, very chubby old monkey matriarch. She sat and watched patiently as this energetic young lady made her way about her new world never bothering to look down or to notice that she was in the company of a new friend. As the baby grew tired of her treetop explorations, she gradually made her way down to the ground. There was her blue wading pool, and there were fresh fruits and vegetables; all of these held her attention, but suddenly the baby noticed there was something else, some*one* else. Suddenly she noticed there was . . . a monkey!

The instant recognition in her eyes was unmistakable. The elderly girl approached the baby; she had a stern, yet gentle, look in her old hazel-colored eyes. Monkey Girl just sat still, more still than I had ever seen her. She was not afraid of anything but she was in awe of this wonderful one who was now standing only inches away from her. The matriarch reached out her soft, wrinkled hand. How long had it been since she had seen such a young one? Had she had babies taken from her love and care? This was for her, too, a moment of recognition and reunion. She uttered a soft mother monkey call. Monkey Girl had no reason to resist, no reason to wait, and in less than a moment she was in her lap, touching her soft cheek, pulling her fur—not the fur of a dog or a kitten, not the soft hair of a pig friend's ear. No, this was monkey fur, this was a mother's fur, this was now *her* mother's fur. Once again by some miracle she was not alone, she was no longer an orphan. All the months of wanting her mother, all the other won-derful animal friends had been generous substitutes but now she had the real thing, the real *one*. And the lone matriarch—she had found a baby.

We cannot know how many thousands of animals suffer every day because of meaningless greed. But we do know that for these two, their days of loneliness are over. These two incredible souls, who had been through more suffering than most of us could bear, now have each other. They spend everyday together in the company of the troupe of old rhesus girls and all now enjoy their life filled with sunshine and rain, with insects and fragrant beds of hay, with oak trees, and most importantly, with freedom from pain and suffering.

Thanks, But No Thanks

If we were asked, most of us would say that we have a favorite animal or at least a favorite species of animal. Some of us favor raccoons, some of us armadillos; some prefer eagles or feel a certain fondness for monkeys. It is often the case that the animals we feel most connected to are animals whom we have read about or had the opportunity to see or even care for. Perhaps this is why dogs and cats are often the first creatures we think of when we say the word "animal."

Wildlife Rescue has, through the many years, done its best to care for an incredibly wide range of wild animals. It has usually been easy to tell their stories and to evoke sympathy and understanding for these amazing creatures. For the most part, all of us have seen a raccoon, opossum, or skunk; we have watched mockingbirds and cardinals flitting about in the trees in our yards and city parks. It seems that the human experience is one that encourages us to feel for what and who we know or are familiar with. But there is an entire population of silent, night-dwelling birds whom few of us have the privilege to ever see, much less really get to know. There was however, a couple in Marion, Texas, who did have the unique opportunity to not only observe but actually save an entire family of these seldom-seen birds.

As you know, spring is the time when all manner of accidents happen to wildlife. While they are doing their best to have and raise their babies, we are doing our best to trim trees, clean out storage sheds and garages, and mow overgrown fields. In these activities, we inadvertently upset and threaten their lives. The spring of 1980 was no exception to these traditional human practices.

There was a majestic old live oak tree living next to a farmhouse just outside of the town of Marion. For countless years this tree had been home to squirrels, mockingbirds, caterpillars, and lizards. This tree also offered a particularly nice, safe hollow for one other animal as well. It was in this particular spring that a pair of screech owls decided to choose the old oak as their home. In no time they had cleaned out the hollow and set about the task of settling in and laying their three eggs. The elderly couple living in the farmhouse was not even aware of the owl family's presence. Every night the parent birds would fly from the hollow and disappear into the night. All of their time was spent hunting food for their babies. On occasion one of the small, slate-gray birds would take advantage of the single, bright, yard light shining over the oak tree attracting juicy nighttime insects. For weeks all went well for the owl family. It was not until an early-morning thunderstorm hit the area with high winds and torrential rains that the owls' life took a turn for the worse. Thunderstorms are a welcome sight during a warm spring; the problem with this one was that it hit during the same predawn hours that the owl family was teaching their youngsters to fly. One by one the fledglings emerged from the hollow. One by one they fluttered to the ground and as they sat, the cooling rains drenched their small, feathered bodies. There was nothing for mom and dad owl to do. They could not retrieve their threatened young. They could only fly to their side or call to them from the safety of the tree, hoping that somehow they could find their way back to the nest. But the baby birds could not fly to safety; they could only sit and wait in the pouring rain.

By the time the sun rose, the young owls' feathers were saturated; the three of them sat shivering and frightened. Their parents had fallen silent. Their overnight vigil had done nothing to save their babies, and now that the sun had risen and there were people walking about, they knew that it was not safe. They dared not fly to the ground; all they could do was watch silently from the top of the old live oak.

It was not until the elderly couple walked outside to assess the storm damage that the baby owls were discovered. It was difficult to believe that the three wet lumps of gray feathers were actually living, breathing babies. The owl parents watched helplessly from the tree as their three offspring were gently picked up, dried off, and placed in a large cardboard box. They watched in silence as their babies disappeared into the old farmhouse, carried away from their sight, carried away with no chance for them to ever reclaim or care for their young again.

Two hours passed before a volunteer from Wildlife Rescue arrived. She had come to pick up the "orphans." Because no one had ever seen the parent screech owls, because no one knew that there was a nest in the hollow of the old tree, it was assumed that the babies had been somehow caught up in the storm and transported to the spot where they were found. The couple looked everywhere for a nest. The volunteer searched the area hoping to discover some trace of the parent birds so that the fledglings could be returned to them, but no human eye could observe the hollow on the opposite side of the majestic oak. No human eye could see the two sad, gray figures sitting quietly watching as their family vanished into the waiting vehicle. To the mother and father screech owls, their babies were not being rescued—they were being stolen. The fact that well-meaning people were stealing them made no difference. All they knew was that their three cherished young were soon to be gone forever and it seemed that all they could do was sit and watch.

We will never know if it was the father or the mother owl who called out, it hardly matters, but just as the volunteer's car pulled out of the yard and headed down the driveway, the elderly woman could not help but hear the loud, plaintive hooting of a hopeful parent owl calling one last time to her young. The calls could not be mistaken and they could not be ignored. They were loud and distinct. They were the calls of a bird who could do little else but who would not sit silently by as she lost her babies.

The volunteer saw the elderly couple waving frantically, turned her car around, and raced the owls back to the yard. Now all eyes were focused on the old oak and in only minutes, where before there had been just dense, green foliage, suddenly there appeared the perfect silhouette of two adult screech swls. Only one challenge remained; how to get the babies and the parents reunited.

In only minutes, a twelve-foot ladder, some baling wire, and some fresh, green alfalfa were gathered together to create the perfect makeshift owl nest. The baling wire served as the handle, the alfalfa the nest material, and the box became the tree hollow. Twelve feet up into the tree was a perfect, strong limb and there the new nest was hung in place. The almost-orphaned babies were gently tucked inside on top of the soft, clean alfalfa. It was time for the humans to step back and watch as nature did her work. From deep inside the cardboard box could be heard the high-pitched hoots of the baby owls; the parent owls wasted no time in flying to their side, first one adult, then the other. Landing on a cardboard nest was not easy; it felt foreign to the parent owls. But strange or not, these two were not about to take any chances. They had their babies back, and in only several minutes, both the mother and father owl had made their way into the new nest.

In the coming weeks, the perfect ending to a near tragedy would unfold. As the baby owls grew, they had little need for their simulated nest. In only days, they were up and perching on the side of the box. From there they once again fluttered to the ground, but this time there was no storm and they were strong enough to make their way into low-lying shrubs and trees. At one point, one youngster was seen back in the tree hollow with one of the parents. And in no time, the three were flying about and perching in the uppermost canopy of that grand old tree. Because there were people who cared, but most of all because there were people who paid attention to nature, the owl family was able to get the help they needed and go on living their life as one of the amazing residents of the majestic old oak.

No Fowl Play
or
This Duck Means Business

As every new morning dawns, it is easy to see that we are completely surrounded by another beautiful and fortunately green summer. Walking about the grounds here at the sanctuary in Kendalia, Texas, my eyes are often met with the site of multiple small flocks of who I like to call, "mixed ducks." These amiable, feathered beings waddle about in their colorful coats of snow white, brown, mixed lush greens, blues, and coal black. They quack and squawk and call to one another creating such a cacophony of sound that at times it is possible only to listen to their conversations instead of having one of your own.

We have been rescuing ducks here at WRR throughout our history. Most have come from private hands, the unknowing public who purchased a fluffy, yellow baby from a roadside vendor or feed store. These babies, along with helpless orphaned chicks, have been exploited for decades; for years they were dyed every hideous color imaginable and were never allowed the loving care of their mothers. They are sold to a public who does not realize that, before what seems like overnight, these precious little ones will grow into mature adults with needs very different from that of a youngster. Ducks are intelligent, curious birds who enjoy the company of other members of their flock and who seek out and need the close-knit relationships that are a natural part of their society. There are ducks who are considered "quackless," ducks who nest in trees, ducks who dive and, as we found out here at WRR, ducks who love cats.

It was many years ago during an early spring rain that a young lady arrived at the sanctuary toting a large, bright pink and green quilt. Anyone arriving at WRR with such a bundle is met with an immediate assumption that someone is hiding in that bundle, someone usually in need of our help. This was no exception. It turns out

49

that in this particular bundle was a tiny yellow fluff of a baby duck. Barely holding on to life, this little one had been purchased as an Easter pet. But it was clear early on that he was in very poor health and most likely would not survive. I was amazed that he had held on as long as he did considering that he was as limp as a wet cloth and felt as if he had been kept in a refrigerator. In the early days of WRR we had only the most essential medical supplies and this little fellow needed everything we could muster to pull him through. Warm fluids and hours spent being turned from side to side on a heating pad were the first order of business to keep this fluffy body and soul together. The duckling's beak had shed almost all its color and his minute, webbed feet no longer held a vibrant orange hue; all his extremities looked pale and hopeless. But there was a determined spirit lurking in this soft, almost lifeless, body and it was this spirit that would find its way to overcome all the terrible events that had occurred in this young life.

By late evening, the duckling was much improved, and two mornings later he was waddling about, picking up small bits of food and preening all that fluffy down. In the coming weeks, as this determined orphan grew into an awkward juvenile, it was clear that he had a unique plan for how he was going to live his life at the sanctuary. On his first outing, we tried to introduce him to the other birds. He would quickly shy away from the chickens, running as fast as his webbed feet would carry him to the safety of the sanctuary house. Even the geese, his closer relative, did not seem to interest him. Every time he lingered in their company, his small duck body was dwarfed even more by their majestic gray and white-feathered mass, and their overpowering honks only drowned out his duckling squeaks. There were only four other ducks who lived at WRR at the time, and they were elderly Muscovy ducks who were close friends and seemed to have no need for a teenager in their clan.

There was, however, a huge male cat named Marmalard living at the sanctuary; he was named Marma*lard* because he was so fat! He was the kindest of kitties, always lying about benignly licking a young raccoon or fostering the occasional opossum; it never seemed to occur to Marmalard to consider any of these animals as food. His girth was a good indication that he had plenty of food provided for him in his very own bowl. And it was that very own bowl that one day caught the eye of the little duckling. He had spent his morning walking about, investigating puddles of water and bits of scratch leftover from the chicken contingency, when suddenly his keen, blue eyes caught sight of a small blue bowl that was sitting in front of a huge yellow cat. Young Duck waddled over to see what was in the bowl and was delighted to find a wonderful thing called cat food. Well, this was indeed a treat, and his dark-orange beak probed every inch of that bowl and removed each tiny morsel. It was only after Young Duck was satisfied that it was all gone that he bothered to introduce himself to Marmalard who had been patiently sitting by watching this uninvited guest devour his lunch. Young Duck looked up and I do believe at that very moment fell in love. He did not need to look any further, for Young Duck had found his best friend.

He immediately began grooming Marmalard with his soft, orange beak—up one side of the cat's rotund body and down the other, collecting so much yellow fur that when he finally paused to draw a breath it looked as if a giant fur ball had exploded in his beak. From that moment on, everywhere that Marmalard went, Young Duck was not far behind. Whenever it rained and the big, yellow cat would squeeze his way through the cat door, right on his tail was Young Duck, waddling his way through the small opening. He loved the rain, but he loved Marmalard even more. Every time someone showed up at the sanctuary with another animal in need of help, there was Marmalard and Young Duck—the official greeting party. Marmalard would rub on their legs, as Young Duck would busily preen Marmarlard while he carried out his duty of welcoming the surprised human. One day we were presented with a situation that showed us all just how strong this bond between the duck and the cat really was.

When WRR was located on our first four acres, we were surrounded by a wide assortment of neighbors. Some of these neighbors kept very large dogs as companions and most were allowed to roam free. Late one autumn afternoon when I was in the old stone house that was our combined nursery and clinic, I heard an awful noise. As I ran to see the cause, I was met with a terrible sight. One of the roaming large dogs had trapped Marmarlard at the base of a huge live oak and was doing his best to kill him. But in the midst of this deadly scene was one more animal. There, holding fast with that bright-orange beak to the huge dog's tail was Young Duck, now a fully mature snow-white, feathered beauty. He clearly was a formidable foe, or at least he thought he was. The big dog was turning and spinning—not knowing exactly what to do—one moment he was catching a cat and the next he was being assaulted from behind by this big brave Young Duck.

As I ran toward the trio screaming, no one except the dog seemed to notice me, for attached to his tail was this large, white duck that he wanted only to be rid of. He looked at me as if to say, "Please get this crazed bird off of me!" but Young Duck would not be trifled with. Once again, that determined spirit that had long ago saved his tiny, limp life was now about to save the life of his best friend, Marmalard the Cat. The large dog somehow broke free of Young Duck's grip and the last I saw of him, he was running non-stop for the safety of his home. Marmalard was badly bruised and traumatized; he was panting and loudly crying out as only a terrified kitty can. But in only a moment Young Duck was there at his side, preening that fat, yellow cat body and letting his best friend know that he had nothing to fear as long as he was around.

A Prickly Friend

In only a few weeks, spring will be tinting the treetops green and the wildflowers once more will cover the Texas landscape. Already the sparrows are flitting about gathering bits of dried grass and discarded feathers to construct this year's nest for their soon-to-be-laid eggs. Baby opossums have bravely ventured out of their mothers' pouches and are clinging tenaciously to their backs. All of these harbingers of spring do not seem quite so real when you look at the calendar hanging on the wall. But today is warm and sunny and if we are hit with an end-of-winter blizzard, as we were over twenty-five years ago, we might be surprised with late-winter, early-spring babies.

In February of 1980, all of Central Texas was enjoying spring-like weather; the days were sunny and breezy, the nights cool and calm. The weather forecasters were confident that the Arctic front that had slammed into the Midwest would have little effect on our part of the world. Not surprisingly, they were mistaken. Early one morning just before daybreak, the wind shifted, and when it did there were no more cool breezes. Now in their place were ice-chilled gusts of no less than thirty miles per hour. The severely cold wind would have been enough to convince us that winter was still present, but Mother Nature decided to send us a generous dose of moisture as well. By mid-morning the trees at the sanctuary were covered in shimmering sheets of ice. San Antonio was not to escape the winter blast. Tree limbs came crashing to the ground, electrical wires were sagging under the weight of the ice, and most major highways were closed. We knew what this meant to the native wildlife. Any babies who were in nests were threatened, especially if their mothers or fathers had met disaster in the storm. We waited for the phones to ring.

The first orphan of the storm was a small, but fully-furred, squirrel. Her nest had fallen to the ground. Mother squirrel had retrieved all of her siblings, but she did not come back for this baby. She was fat and healthy so we knew that she would be fine, and in only a few weeks could once again go free. Five more baby squirrels came in that same day. At least now we had a complete family who could grow up as siblings. The most unusual baby in need of rescue was yet to come.

In late February, even in very cold winters, we were accustomed to rescuing baby squirrels and baby opossums. Raccoons, skunks, bobcats, and foxes rarely give birth in the winter, but this new baby was a member of a species we had only rescued once before, and that was in the middle of summer. There was no way of knowing exactly what had happened to mom, but when this tiny baby was found wandering in a backyard in far northwest San Antonio, it was clear that she was cold and hungry. The young man who brought the help-less infant porcupine to us was not certain whom he had rescued. He first thought that this was someone's "pet" hedgehog. The little baby's paws were frozen, her quills were coated with ice, and her soft dark eyelashes closed tightly over her small round eyes. Her breath was shallow and barely noticeable. We had little hope for her survival but she was young and if she had not been away from her mom too long, she just might have a chance.

After three long hours spent sleeping on a heating pad, the baby porcupine was showing signs of recovery. Within two more hours the frozen baby was up and waddling about. At least now we had warm fluids to give the waiting youngster. Now she was able to burrow slowly into the soft alfalfa bed we had prepared for her. High-pitched, yet barely audible, pitiful-sounding cries were her only form of pro-test. This baby was weak and frightened. By late that evening, the porcupine was reasonably stable, but she needed to be bottle-fed. She was still nursing when her mom disappeared, and now we had to con-tinue the process. The only problem was that the baby knew full well that we were not her mother.

Trying to bottle-feed a baby porcupine, quills and all, who does not want to be fed is a challenge. Little by little, she learned to tolerate us. Porcupines are docile animals, but like all wild animals they would prefer not to be bothered by humans. The most important issue for this little female was to help her reach a stage where she could feed herself. This way, she would not be stressed by our presence and she would not become dangerously dependent on our help. By mid-March the female porcupine was able to lap formula from a shallow bowl and she was slowly beginning to chew on the plants and vegetables pro-vided for her. In the wild, porcupines develop very rapidly, but this baby had a slow and dangerous beginning. In addition, she had to deal with the fact that she was the only one of her kind in our care. It was not likely that we would be rescuing any more porcupines, so we decided to find someone who could serve as a suitable companion.

Living at WRR that same winter was a rather old, large, brown, domestic rabbit. He was the only domestic rabbit at the sanctuary and he, too, had no companions. The day we introduced the dissimilar two we were not exactly optimistic that they would get along. The big, brown rabbit was released into the porcupine's small, indoor enclosure; he immediately hopped over to investigate the strange, quilled resident. The bunny sniffed then quickly jumped back. The porcupine called out in her plaintive tone. The old, brown rabbit stopped, and his ears leaned slowly forward; the porcupine's cry is not unlike the cry of a rabbit. Now the rabbit seemed less threatened by the quilled youngster. It was clear that the young porcupine wanted the rabbit's attention. The rabbit simply had to relax; the porcupine would do the rest. The old, brown rabbit lay down on his side, his ears back; he was now more curious than afraid. The young porcupine waddled over and began nudging into the rabbit's soft fur. The rabbit's long whiskers twitched, his nose wiggled; he had changed his mind about his new companion. By nightfall, the two were comfortable in each other's company. By the end of the week they were inseparable.

Thanks to the companionship and care from the elderly rabbit, the young porcupine learned to care for herself. She was grasping chunks of fresh carrot and apple in her once-frozen paws, and she was agilely browsing through piles of tender green foliage. She climbed to the top of the sturdy oak branches in the enclosure, as the brown rabbit remained content on the ground feeding on fresh, green alfalfa. The docile porcupine who had once teetered on the edge of death was now strong, fat, and full of life. It was time for her to return to her world.

The spring weather had settled in, the trees were vibrant green and the every inch of earth was covered once again with bright flowers and soft grass. The ice of previous months had melted and the sun was warming every new day. An early morning in mid-April was chosen as the day to set the porcupine free. As we approached the enclosure we could hear her distinct cries. In only minutes we would learn why she was in distress. Sometime during the night the old brown rabbit had died. The porcupine was nudging at his fur and getting no response. These two very different animals had grown to care for one another, had spent months in each other's company and now the younger of the two was to go free while the elder had died and found his way to the ultimate freedom. We left the two together for a time and decided that it was best to go ahead with our plans.

As we arrived at the release site, the porcupine was sitting quietly in her carrier. There were tall trees and dense underbrush. There was a nearby river and three quiet ponds. Other porcupines had often been seen here and this would now be her world, too. The door to her carrier was opened and, with that familiar waddle, she made her way out of the carrier across the narrow pasture and into the densely wooded acreage. She did not look back or utter a cry. She simply made her way back into her world. I do not doubt that forever in her memory will remain the gentle companionship of one elderly brown rabbit who shared her world for a brief while and made her days as a captive a little easier to bear.

Seeing with New Eyes

It seems to me that it is all too easy to take animals for granted. Those of us who are fortunate to live in the company of dogs and/or cats see them every day; we feed them, brush them, take them to the vet, fuss at them when they annoy us, chastise them when they do something we perceive to be wrong. Usually until their later years we assume they will always be around, always be a part of our lives.

On a larger scale, our society views animals as voiceless, emotionless creatures living their lives with an utter lack of desire, needs, or reason. I have often wondered what would happen if one day everyone decided to spend one week of their life quietly observing a backyard full of birds, or followed their beloved companion animal about doing as the animal does, walking, scratching, napping, simply being. Or really getting to know a cow or sheep or a chicken. Perhaps ancient, now sleeping sensitivities would once again awaken in us. I firmly believe our lives would be enhanced. If we were keen observers what would we see; how would we label what our eyes and hearts took in? Would we become uncomfortable if we noticed similarities between the animals' behavior and our own? We are, after all, members of the animal kingdom. I imagine that if we were wise enough to draw parallels between human and non-human animal behavior there would be less "managing," killing, and exploiting of the animal kingdom. Perhaps we would stop believing it is acceptable to "break" horses, "manage" herds, and factory "farm" cows.

I was trying my best to explain this to a gentleman who called Wildlife Rescue last month. He called us because he wanted WRR to send someone out to remove every squirrel that lived or even traveled through his one dozen or so block neighborhood. It is a small area, he told me, so why not just come out, set several traps and catch the "little rodents," as he liked to refer to them. He told me how he dearly loved to sit and watch the birds come to his feeders; they gave him such joy and they are so beautiful to watch, he explained. I asked him if he could imagine seeing the same beauty and finding the same joy in the squirrels. "Absolutely not!" was his adamant response. "These squirrels are nothing but a nuisance!" He was quite clear—he wanted them removed and he expected us to carry out the nasty deed.

It is important to understand that we try to adhere to a policy at WRR. Our policy is that we do our best to help every caller in some way or another. It is not uncommon that our way of helping is to educate. I cannot tell you how many times over the past 20+ years we have encountered callers who simply do not want to be educated, and I can assure you this gentleman was one of them. Wildlife Rescue does not believe it is in any healthy, wild animal's best interest to be removed from the area she calls home. We do not believe in live-trapping urban wild animals and taking them away from known food sources, family members, and a comfortable, familiar life simply because we human animals have decided that they are a nuisance. So when someone calls us and asks us to remove every squirrel in the neighborhood, then we feel it is time to educate, even though we are often confronted with an unwilling "student."

We were particularly concerned with this situation because we knew that mother squirrels were already setting up housekeeping and babies were not far behind, if in fact not already on the scene. I did everything I could to convince our caller to leave the squirrels alone; I told him to take a close look at their endearing faces, to watch them at play, to get to know them. I knew anyone who loved birds surely could be a squirrel convert as well. But our caller would have none of it. He threatened to put out poison, to shoot the squirrels, to set up steel jaw traps in his trees. This guy was definitely a tough customer. I kept talking, buying time with every conversation. Little did I know things were going to get stickier before they got better.

Why is it that the rain and wind so often come just when you don't need them, or at least when you think you don't need them. Two or three days passed and our gentleman friend had not called. I had not called him because with the rain and wind, babies were starting to come in at the sanctuary, and as you might have guessed they were almost all squirrel babies. I hated to think what was going on in our caller's neighborhood if he had made good on even one of his threats. I decided to gather up my courage and call him. As "luck" would have it, just the night before the wind had brought down a mother squirrel's nest, babies and all right in his backyard. I anxiously inquired about the babies, half-holding my breath. He did not mince words; he had them and he was going to kill them, all four of them. I told him to please just set them outside, their mother would come and get them; if she did not then we would send someone over and pick them up. "No ma'am," was his reply, if he could not get rid of all the squirrels, at least he could get rid of these four babies. I could not talk fast enough or say anything to convince him. I tried to appeal to his sympathy for the innocent pink babies, but he only slammed the phone down. Fortunately, we ask for the address of every caller, so we knew how to find our friend and hopefully we could get to his house in time to save the squirrels.

When our volunteer arrived, he could get no response; no one answered the door and he could find no trace of a nest nor could he find any neighbors who knew of the caller's whereabouts. I felt sure that we had failed; not only had we not educated, we had alienated someone and ultimately had lost the lives of four animals. I could feel little other than pity for this unknown man; he seemed so sad to me. How could he love birds and hate squirrels? Why is it that animals have to be the way we think they should be before we can consider them worthy of our respect? Why is it so easy for us to pick our favorite species, instead of seeing the beauty in all of them?

I waited until the next day around noon then decided it was worth one more try. I had all my speeches ready; I knew just what I was going to say when he answered the phone. I was ready to be as accommodating as I could to talk him into letting those babies live. The phone rang three times before he answered. I apologized for bothering him but asked if there was some way we could possibly get the four baby squirrels. His reply was brief and to the point as always. "You are too late, I have already taken care of the problem." I asked him what he had done. "Well, I put them outside like you told me to!" Suddenly his voice softened, "And you will not believe what happened!" Our gentleman caller went on and on. "That momma squirrel came down out of that big, old, oak tree and sniffed around; she ran back up the tree when I tried to go near her, so I let her be. She came back in only a few minutes, sniffed some more, grabbed one of those tiny, tiny babies in her mouth, and up the tree she took off like a shot. I couldn't believe how fast she could run with that baby in her mouth. And you know she came back for each one of those babies. I have never seen anything like it in my life. I always thought squirrels were just dirty rodents. I have never seen anything like this in my life." He went on and on about how the mother looked thin and so he decided to set up a squirrel feeder. He talked about how she had quite a job ahead of her raising a family of four all by herself. So he thought that he should help out in any way he could. We talked about what squirrels like to eat and how soon the babies would leave their nest and how he could look forward to watching them grow up right there in his backyard. There was no more discussion of traps, of poison, no thought of harming or killing; just a simple, important revelation and appreciation of life in all the amazing, beautiful forms it takes. Thanks to that beauty, somewhere in San Antonio there is a small, quiet, tree-studded neighborhood where the natural devotion of a mother squirrel opened the eyes of an elderly gentleman who sits quietly watching her care for her young.

Strength in Timidity

Once, many years ago, Wildlife Rescue was called on to help save dozens of monkeys who had been confined in a woman's basement in Iowa. As you can imagine, suddenly being called on to take well over a dozen primates is quite a challenge. But we had been rescuing primates for many years and these animals were in particularly dire straits, so we felt it was critical to do whatever we could to make certain they did not find themselves in the hands of another collector.

Many of the monkeys were ill, some were elderly, and all were in need of fresh air, sunshine, and a nutritious diet. The individual who had the animals had continued to get more and more of them until her entire house was filled with cages full of monkeys. After she showed up at her veterinarian's office repeatedly with dying primates, he decided it was time to contact the local health department. When the authorities arrived, they were barely able to spend ten minutes in the house before the odors of urine and feces overwhelmed them. By the time Wildlife Rescue was contacted, the monkeys had been confiscated and were in the care of the veterinarian at the local university. Dr. Paul Cooper called us in the hope that we could either place the monkeys or bring them to the sanctuary. We decided to have most of the primates brought to Wildlife Rescue. There were some whom we did not have room for and we were very grateful for the invaluable help that PAWS (Performing Animal Welfare Society) in Galt, California, provided by taking in some of the monkeys at their sanctuary.

There was a great deal of paperwork to process and many details to take care of before the monkeys were freed from their life of abuse. The only positive element about this was that the delays provided the time we needed to construct the spacious enclosures that would be their new homes. When building a new home for any animal, you think first, last, and always of how the animal or animals live in the wild. You mimic their natural habitat the best you can: make it as tall, wide, and interesting as you can, and hope they will find some peace and enjoyment living there. For these monkeys in particular, we imagined what their lives had been like living in a sealed house with no fresh air, no sunshine, surrounded by filth. We knew we had to do everything in our power to make their new home a true sanctuary. For weeks we worked hard constructing the new enclosure. We surrounded a stand of four oak trees, knee high native grasses, rocks, and shrubs, then topped the eighteen-foot-high enclosure, and waited for our new residents to arrive. Finally the day came and literally crate after crate of primates arrived at the airport. The crates were small so all you could see were these tiny, terrified faces peering out from behind the screens. We opened the small sliding hatches on the front of each crate to hand them welcomed pieces of juicy oranges and grapes. One by one, the most petite, sometimes shaky, yet perfect hands and nimble fingers reached out to take the nutritious treats. It was a sunny, breezy day—the perfect weather for liberating mistreated animals and introducing them to a new and better life.

We positioned the crates just inside of the new enclosure. Slowly we unlatched each hook and slid open the door to each compartment of every crate. At least these monkeys had all lived in the same small room at their former "home"; this told us they were compatible and would continue to enjoy being in each other's company. Even though the doors were now open, there was little activity. The monkeys inside were no doubt afraid, cautious, and somewhat overwhelmed by their new surroundings. Minutes passed and finally one brave, timid, little captive emerged from her crate. She was a white-fronted capuchin— frail, thin, and missing most of the hair on her back and stomach. Her eyes were sad; she was solemn and so quiet for a monkey. Soon she was followed by one of her companions, another capuchin, only this young male was not so timid. He took his time coming out of the crate, but once free of the dark box he began bounding about the enclosure. He ran around touching every blade of grass he could reach and on his way up into one of the oak trees he grabbed sticks and chunks of tall succulent weeds. Once he settled on one of the oak branches he just could not wait to investigate his new treasures. As he picked through the sticks and foliage, the timid female joined him. She seemed impressed with his courage and took comfort sitting by his side on the rough tree branch. Once the other monkeys realized it was safe to come out, there were primates pouring out of every open door. In what now seems like seconds, the newly rescued monkeys were searching about their new home, finding pieces of nature that before now had probably faded into a dim, pleasant memory. We watched as these intelligent, abused creatures took their places in their new life.

But suddenly we realized someone was missing. There in the very last crate, the door propped wide open, was an elderly cinnamon capuchin. He looked like he must be the eldest of the entire clan. It seemed that all of the other monkeys had forgotten him in all of the excitement. He sat in the doorway of the crate, looking out onto the scene of all his companions now sitting in the fresh air, soaking up the warm sunshine, feasting on slices of bananas, oranges, whole, purple grapes, and juicy tomatoes. He appeared to be almost frozen there in that tiny doorway. We offered him some of the precious fruit, but all he would do was stare down at his bowl. What could be going through his mind? Why would he not come out and enjoy this wonderful new environment? An hour passed, then two, then three. Nothing changed; he just sat and sat and stared. It would be dark soon; we did not want to just leave him there, alone in an unfamiliar home, sitting in that dark, awful crate. But there was little we could do. We had to hope that his "family" would take care of him or that he would gain the courage needed to come out and take his place amongst the others.

We checked on the elderly monkey several times that night. He finally fell asleep in his crate. There he lay by himself as all the other monkeys bedded down under the stars. It was so sad to see this old fellow, all alone, too afraid to even enjoy the fact that finally he had a life worth living. Perhaps one of the other monkeys agreed with us that something had to be done. We would never have guessed who it would be. Tiny though she was, she must have known what it was like to be so afraid you can barely move because early the very next morning that tiny, timid female capuchin made her way over to the elderly monkey's crate. In her petite, frail hands she held one of the last pieces of fresh, juicy orange left over from the feast the others had enjoyed just the day before. Her hand was so tiny that the orange wedge covered it entirely while the sweet juice was dripping through her fingers. She oh-so-gently placed the fruit just outside the door of his crate. Slowly, the almost naked, but still handsome, head of a very old, very tired male monkey emerged. He looked down at the orange and then he gazed over at the little girl monkey waiting there, coaxing him with her eyes, her soft chirps to please come out and join the others. Surely she must be telling him it was finally safe, that finally there was a reason to come out, that there were things he must see, things he would love, things he had probably not seen for countless years. Somehow, as only one such as she could, she convinced him. That old male monkey came out into the bright morning sunshine and when he did, there were the others to greet him and assure him that all was well and safe and new. The young males looked on from the tops of the oak trees. They tossed bits of dark-green leaves down on him, and he picked them up from the soft, brown dirt and sniffed them. He touched rocks and weeds and bark and insects; he smelled everything he touched. The old male's eyes brightened with every step he took and with each step, the frail, timid female was at his side. She had been the first one to emerge from her crate. She had been too afraid to even take three steps out into the enclosure, but she could not sit idly by when the elderly male needed her most.

With her help, over the coming weeks, he would learn to enjoy his new life. Often you could find them sitting high in the oak tree, sharing a meal of leaves and fresh fruit; thanks to her, he had made his way into this new and oh-so-better life. And on the morning that we found him dead, it was the timid, little, girl capuchin monkey who was there by his side. She was still the shyest one of them all, but she had been his strength; she had stayed by his side to make sure he did not miss one single day of his new life. For all of the years of abuse, at least for awhile he had her and a fine new home to live out his days, to hopefully forget the cruel, dark past and live even those brief months in the newfound warmth of the bright sunshine.

They Never Gave Up

You could probably ask anyone who works as an intern, volunteer, or staff at Wildlife Rescue and they would all tell you there are no dull moments here. If anything, we offer our fine, hard-working people plenty of excitement, and all in the name of saving animals. What could be a better way to make a living?

The excitement started one day when we received a call about some domestic ducks who were doing their best to carry out a peaceful life on a suburban park pond. Sadly, there were some individuals in this same suburb who had other ideas for these peace-loving water birds. A concerned caller told us that they had seen two ducks who had arrows piercing their necks and heads but were somehow managing to survive.

Staff member Rob Koger went to the rescue of the troubled fowl to see if he could capture the birds and bring them to the sanctuary for help.

Rob arrived in late afternoon and found that there was a construction fence surrounding the pond, but a section of the fencing had been torn away so that people could come and go in the area. There were well over three-dozen Peking, Muskovy, and Muskovy/Mallard ducks living on this mid-sized lake, and most were ready to settle in for the evening. As he surveyed the area, Rob noticed that about 100 yards from him was a small, quiet gathering of feathered friends and there in the midst of these was one of the wounded birds. With net in hand, Rob ever so slowly approached the resting, yet agile, duck and gently captured and carefully placed him in a carrier. On closer examination, the arrows that had been shot into this bird looked almost like heavy bolts possibly coming from a hand-held crossbow.

By this time, Rob was confident that good fortune was on our side. The other duck could not be far away, and on into the rapidly approaching dusk he went to find the little fellow. After a long, hopeful walk around the grassy bank, Rob spotted the second abused bird. This poor soul had not gotten off so easily; he had been shot at least three times as there were three arrows in his neck and upper shoulders. But remarkably, he too was alert and agile. He was in fact so agile and so intent on not being helped that he would have no part in our plans to save his life. As Rob approached, once again with net in hand, to carry out his good deed, the beautiful brown and dark green bird, accompanied by his friends, gracefully slipped into the safety of the dark water.

How often do we assume that humans alone show compassion to one another, help one another when sick, injured, or in trouble? And yet, here on this pond were two ducks with two very important things in common: they had been assaulted and were in need of help. Someone had come along and either tried to kill them or simply found "sport" in using them for target practice. No one knows how long they sat and swam and did their best to eat with these arrows piercing their heads. They had come to know this pond as home, this pond where they lived with their companions, their loyal companions who knew that they were in trouble but would not leave them alone to suffer and die, who instead kept constant company with them. When the evasive green and brown bird used the pond as his only escape route, he was never alone—there by his side were his buddies watching, swimming, staying close even with the imminent threat of being captured by a member of the very species that had harmed them, still they would not leave their fellows.

After several valiant but failed attempts, Rob decided to come back and try another day. For the remainder of this night, the ducks would once again have their peace and quiet, their time to be together to swim quietly under the crescent moon, to groom and preen their soft, dense feathers, to bury their heads under their wings and find the peacefulness of a good night's sleep. For one more night, the injured bird would be accepted into the clutch of his dozing friends, not realizing that this would be his last evening in their company. The following afternoon, Rob was once again at the pond and once again the agile duck was ready to do all in his power to avoid being captured. As the evening wore on, our feathered friends decided to bed down along the grassy banks not quite so near the water as before. It was growing darker by the minute, but not being one to give up easily, Rob persevered in his pursuit of the determined bird. A slow, quiet, and steady approach with a well-focused lunge seemed the only way to assure success. In a flurry of feathers and frightened squawking, the poor, traumatized birds scattered for their lives, never knowing that this persistent human was not out to harm them. Somehow, in all the darkness and chaos of attempted flight, Rob had managed to perfectly position his net so that the targeted duck was now captured and safely in a carrier.

Once here at the clinic, all the wretched arrows were removed, the ducks who would not give up their lives to this cruelty were cared for, and in only a few weeks were recovering beautifully and ready to go outside in the duck and chicken yard. Today, these two beautiful birds go about their days swimming in the wading pools, visiting with their new companions, quacking and eating and carrying on as if they were never used as targets.

We can never know what goes on in the sensitive, intelligent minds of animals who are so horribly treated. But we can trust, by what we see here at WRR every day, that they are strong and brave and seem to accept gallantly the fact that we clumsy, and sometimes cruel, humans are their neighbors. It seems to me that these incredible creatures we call animals have a depth of understanding that I can only hope to achieve and sensitivity that I find inspiring. If one day we humans learn to share in the peace these animals most surely feel, then we will no longer live in a world where ducks must dodge arrows and wonder if the approaching human is friend or foe.

Gentle "Bear"

As we celebrate each anniversary of helping animals, it is natural to look back, to remember animals both human and non-human, to reflect on why some things happened, to mourn, to be thankful, and to plan ahead.

Wildlife Rescue is evolving into the very organization that I had always dreamed it would. I remember well those difficult days in the late 1970s when all WRR could do was manage to exist day to day, but always present was the very real dream of a beautiful 200–acre sanctuary. Now we are literally living and building that dream. But, as with so many things in life, along with dreams and plans there are often aspects of sadness. Growth and change are funny things. We usually look forward to them, fear them, get excited about them, welcome them, and dread them all at the same time. But one thing is certain: with life comes change and with change, if we are wise, comes growth.

The most important component of Wildlife Rescue is that we save the lives of animals who otherwise would most likely perish. Many of the animals we care for are brought to us by people who found them in dire need of help, hit by a car, poisoned, or trapped. Some are found motherless, lying on the ground waiting to die; then there are those who are left at our gate, tied there with a note, hoping that we will help. This was how Macy the Dog came our way.

It was not long after Wildlife Rescue moved to our twenty-one-acre site just outside of Boerne, Texas. Those, too, were exciting times of change and growth. It was 1987; we had experienced a devastating flood in the early summer of 1986, and we had little more than the bare minimum of land, cages, food, and shelter for the animals in our care. Times were hard then, but as an interesting result of the flood, we were able to purchase the twenty-one acres, which at the time, was the answer to a prayer. Our days were filled with settling in at the new property, getting the house set up with our office, and trying to raise funds to build new enclosures (some things never change!).

I do not remember who found her and brought her in from the road, but all of a sudden there was this frightened yellow dog standing in front of me. She had been tied to the entrance gate with a note, this part I do remember. It went something like this:

> This is Macy; she is part coyote and part dog—a coy-dog. I cannot take care of her. She is a good dog, but she will not stay in my yard. I know this is not the right thing to do, but I hope you can give her a good home.

We were not prepared to take in a dog, especially one who would probably be very unpredictable, but it was obvious that Macy needed a home. We hoped she would get along with the only other dog living at the sanctuary at the time. His name was Bear; he was a great, woolly, black dog with the sweetest disposition, and as it turned out, just who Macy needed.

It took little time to realize that Macy was not comfortable with her new surroundings. She was skittish and shy and not at all sure she did not want to bite anyone who approached her. We offered her a bowl of dog food, tried to comfort her, and introduced her to Bear. Bear walked up to Macy, sniffed in true dog fashion, slowly wagged his tail, and in the language spoken only by dogs, told her she was home. Macy responded by becoming Bear's constant companion. She decided to trust only him, to eat only when he was near, and to stay far away from all humans. Because there was so much constant activity near the house, Macy made her home on the other side of the pond, well beyond our sights and sounds. She would not come up for food, so every day we walked down to the pond with her lunch. As we approached, Macy would slink back into the dense stand of junipers, watch as we placed the familiar bowl of food down for her approval, wait for Bear to give her the "all's clear" tail wag and then, after we had walked the required distance away, out she would come to dine with her trusted friend. This ritual went on for over six weeks. We all worried about her but knew that Bear was doing a good job of watching over Macy.

The two became permanent fixtures beside the pond; you could look out the kitchen window any time of day and there the two companions would be, lying in the sun side by side. WRR only had about a dozen or so ducks in our care at the time and I often worried that

I would find one dead now that Macy was living at the sanctuary, but she never misbehaved; she did not chase the ducks or bark at the other animals. It was clear that Bear was a good influence on her and that she understood that she had found a home, but that in order to stay here she had to fit in with the other animals in our care.

The weeks passed quickly; we were all very busy building new enclosures, and animals were coming in daily. Finally the new sanctuary was beginning to take shape. We had decided that Macy would never come up to the house; she seemed content to live by the pond. Bear would come in the house; he loved the attention of the volunteers, but Macy was just not interested. One afternoon while we were out feeding the ducks we could not help but notice that something was different. It was Macy; she was nowhere to be found. We walked every square inch of the property; we called, we took bowls of fresh meat out hoping the smell would attract her attention and bring her out of hiding. But it was all in vain. Macy had vanished. The shy, frightened dog we had grown to love at a distance had decided to move on. Already we missed the familiar sight of Macy and Bear by the pond. We had to remind ourselves that it was no longer necessary to serve lunch on the banks of the pond. We took great comfort in the fact that Bear was still with us, until three days later when he disappeared. Now we were beginning to suspect foul play. Bear never wandered out of sight; he was such a homebody. Was he so upset at Macy's leaving that he decided to do the same? Three long days and nights passed. We had alerted everyone in the area that we were missing two dogs, yet we had little hope of Macy letting anyone catch her. But surely Bear would welcome anyone's affection.

Day four and still no sign; no word of our missing friends. We were trying to talk ourselves into accepting the worst; they were both gone for good, no explanation, just forever gone. The best thing to do was to get back to work, to focus on the animals who needed us most, to go on and do what had to be done at the sanctuary. Fortunately there was plenty to be done; it was the time of year when animals were coming in faster than we could count. One afternoon an entire family drove up to the sanctuary: five little towheaded children and one very frantic mother. One of the little boys had found an injured opossum who had been hit by a car and was bleeding from the mouth. The children were crying and the mom was hoping we could do something not only to help the injured opossum but to calm her children and assure them that the injured animal would recover. As we examined the opossum, we could find no broken bones; there was an excellent chance he would be just fine. As we worked to reassure the family, one of the little girls slipped out the front door. Her mother told her to please come back in as she was not supposed to be walking around on the sanctuary grounds. The little girl pleaded with her mom, "All I want to do is sit here and pet these two pretty puppies." Puppies? What puppies, I thought—could it be, could she be talking about our long lost dogs? I stepped out onto the front porch and there, dirty, tired, and more beautiful than ever, lay Bear. And who was at his side but the shy, skittish Macy. Had Bear gone away in search of Macy? You will never convince me of anything different. He went out in search of her and he brought her back home. Finally Bear and Macy were home to stay.

Over the years, Bear and Macy became known as regulars at WRR. They would bark an occasional friendly greeting; once in a rare while they would playfully chase a peacock but, all in all, they were two fine and well-behaved friends. It was not until many years later that Bear took ill; we never knew exactly how old he was as he too had come to us as a rescue. But when it came time for him to pass on he did so with great dignity and in his favorite spot, down by the pond. Macy mourned the death of her friend for many weeks. She would go and lie near his favorite place; she moped about the sanctuary, she would not eat, and she was not interested in being comforted by any of us. She just wanted her Bear back. Perhaps it was because she was so lonely that weeks later she was eager to welcome another new friend who needed our help. A massive Great Pyrenees, Angus, had been found roaming down the middle of McCullough Avenue in San Antonio, a bright red sports car honking behind him in afternoon traffic. He was a giant, matted, confused mess. He did not seem to understand why that little red car would not just go around him. He barely fit into the cab of the small, yellow pickup truck I was driving, but he was so grateful for some relief from that annoying sports car that he managed to squeeze in beside me. By the look of his coat and the size of his appetite he had been wandering the streets of San Antonio for some time. All inquiries failed to produce an "owner," so WRR was to become his home.

Angus and Macy became the best of friends. Angus was loving and calm and loyal; he adored Macy and she returned his affection. For over eight years, Angus and Macy were the housedogs at the Boerne sanctuary. Everyone who met them loved them. The two dogs enjoyed swimming in the pond in the hot summer months and they were the benign but serious guard dogs late into the evenings while staff was busy caring for the wild animals. They were the first ones to dart into the house when a thunderstorm would roll out of the clouds and soak the sanctuary with welcome rains.

Over the years, Macy learned to not only tolerate us but to enjoy our company and turn to us for affection. She became great friends with all of the staff and for most of her life seemed to leave behind her wilder, less trusting ways. But as she aged, Macy did as many of us do. She became less tolerant of people, seeming to take comfort in spending most of her days sleeping under the bamboo in the cool, brown soil. She would not always welcome pats on the head and as she developed arthritis, perhaps she felt it was to best to keep to herself. She no longer greeted people bringing animals to the sanctuary, unless it was to let them know that she was not looking for their affection. The staff became her trusted family; we knew her well and loved her deeply.

Macy never liked thunderstorms, in fact she was quite afraid of them. Perhaps that is why it seemed even more tragic that it was the morning after a severe storm that we found her body lying still in front of the sanctuary house. It seemed that she had died in her sleep. Those of us who knew and loved her choose to believe that she died well before the storm was under way. But no matter, when she passed out of this world, what we will cherish most is our fond and loving memories of a rare and special dog named Macy who came to us one day because someone was not able to care for her. The person who left her may never know what a wonderful gift they chained to our gate that day long ago, but we know, and we will always be grateful to them for our wonderful friend named Macy.

Determined to Survive

Suddenly it is spring once again. Only weeks ago the rains came every few days, the skies were gray, cold, and cloudy, and the trees were bare. Now the sky is vibrant blue, little rain graces our days, the trees and grasses are bright green and soft and full with new life.

Wild animals in need of help have been finding their way to our doors. Every day it seems another peaceful, green space falls helpless before the blade and bulldozer. Where are the animals supposed to go when we relentlessly destroy their homes? How do we expect them to survive, or do we expect them to? Do we think of them at all when we decide to create one more housing development on a once peaceful stretch of nature?

On Easter Sunday I was sitting in my car just outside of Boerne, off of IH 10 West. I was waiting for members of my family, and I could not help but notice a huge earthmoving/destroying machine parked in what used to be a green, tree-covered pasture. For some reason, the machine and its driver had stopped just short of the one remaining mid-sized tree; all other lives had been crushed and piled up in a now-smoldering heap. I stared at this tree, a tangle of grapevines coursing through its branches, and suddenly I noticed movement in the dark green canopy. There in that lone surviving tree was a common scene. A pair of cardinals was diligently working to build their new nest. First the female would fly out of the tree, return with some grand treasure in the form of a piece of dried grass or brightly colored string, then the male would emerge, fly out of sight and return with an unidentifiable piece of fluff. I could only imagine that this slice of nature had for some years been their traditional home. Very likely there had been generations of cardinals raised in this very tree and in many others in this now vacant meadow. The beautiful red, top-notched birds seemed to have decided to go forward with their plans no matter what disaster humankind could dish out.

We have no way of knowing how many millions of animals repeat this scene every day. We have no way of knowing how many others do not even get the opportunity to try to carry on with the lives that nature has dictated to them for countless generations. How many billions of animals lose their lives every day on this earth? For those of us who wince every time a butterfly hits our windshield, there is a day-to-day sense of this universal loss of life. Here at Wildlife Rescue, there are daily reminders of this. Since late March the numbers of incoming sick, orphaned, and injured babies have been increasing daily. One night we received over twenty opossums; all of them had lost their mothers. The baby squirrels have been in need of our help since late winter and even now, although it is early in the season, we are receiving orphaned raccoons.

What happened to all of these babies' mothers? What happened to the once-safe nest sites where they were warm and comfortable and cared for? Some years ago when we received an entire litter of gray foxes we knew exactly what had happened. Once upon a time, there was a quiet, lush green space surrounding, of all things, a rock quarry in the middle of San Antonio. This oasis had been a piece of history not only for the city but more importantly for generations of wild birds, mammals, and reptiles. Then one day the world came to an abrupt and violent end for all the residents of that safe island. It seems that the quarry had been sold and the developers had plans of their own for the trees, rocks, caverns, and ponds that the animals called home. The bulldozers moved in, the trees came down, the dense underbrush was scraped away, roots and all, and huge fires were set to finish it off. There was no evidence that anyone had survived the destruction, not until the slightest whimper was heard from deep under a huge boulder. A construction worker knew something terrible had happened, even more terrible than the brutal killing of the green space, if that was possible. As he dug beneath the rock, he saw a thick, bushy, gray tail. He pulled on the fur but there was no response—the tail belonged to a now dead mother fox. But still he could hear the cries deeper beneath the soil. Soon he uncovered enough dirt to discover a litter of tiny, helpless, frightened gray foxes, their mother now dead, crushed by the huge, blind machines. When he brought the foxes to Wildlife Rescue, I asked him if he would let me come to the site just in case there were more animals who could still be found. I will never forget that sight: everywhere I looked there were huge piles of old oak, beautiful pecan, and hackberry trees.

There were agarita bushes, wild grape, and blackberry vines, all of them now uprooted and dying. And there were bodies—raccoons, armadillos, and roadrunners—the earthmovers hadn't missed many. The infant foxes were fortunate to be alive.

The three siblings stayed in our care for over six months. They were healthy and strong and little by little they managed to overcome the challenge of being reared by humans. They played as young foxes do; they always slept in a pile, the largest of the three on the bottom, supporting his two sisters. Did they remember the terrible day when their mother was killed in their den? Did they remember the sounds of the machines coming closer and closer, moving like an earthquake into their world and changing it forever? That is something we will never know; that is something we cannot know. But we do know that everyday more animals die than any of us can dare to imagine. We do know that as the one species that is responsible for so much destruction, we must find a way to be better, to do better, to live lives that do less harm. It is true that we have only one planet, but even if we had a dozen would that be any reason to destroy even one of them?

When the day came to let the foxes go, I knew they could never go back to their home. For their home was now someone else's home, and they would never be tolerated there. We took them far away from any city, far away from any road, and on the day they were set free, as they sniffed the grass and climbed gracefully over the logs and rocks, perhaps they did not remember their old home, but I remembered it. I remembered it as it once was, and I knew it would never be there for them or any other fox ever again.

The Sweetest Flower

Many winters have come and gone since 1977 when Wildlife Rescue was founded. It is truly astounding how quickly time moves through our lives. How rapidly the years flow past, and how little we are aware of this passing until one day we stop, look back, and immediately grab hold of the perspective that shakes us and wakes us to the reality of how short our time here on Earth really is. For me, looking back includes memories of animals who have changed my life every step of the way over the years.

Because WRR has so much to be thankful for these days, I often catch myself remembering the early days in that small, two-bedroom house in San Antonio. Our nearly two-hundred acres was but a dream then, a very well thought-out dream, but hardly more than the faith that one day it would be ours. In the late 1970s, time was filled with an early morning paper route, days of phone calls, animal rescues all over the city, and struggling to raise funds to keep WRR going, growing, and on solid footing for the future. It was not long after the word went out to veterinarians, "pest" control companies, police and fire departments, tree trimmers, and the all-important media, that the calls began coming in. There were the usual opossum-in-the-trash-can calls, the raccoons in the attic, the deer eating the rosebushes, but there was one call regarding a rather unusual little animal.

Most of us know how prevalent the trade in wildlife has been for too many years and how Texas has always been a hotbed of activity in this very cruel business. It was particularly popular in those days for breeders and pet shops to sell "pet" skunks—defenseless little guys who had been stripped of their scent glands and marketed as great household companions. The call came in one cool and breezy Saturday afternoon. A young woman had purchased a skunk from a pet shop and after about three months of trying to make her fit in with her dogs and cats, realized that she had made a terrible mistake. I told her to bring the skunk to me and, knowing she could never be set free, I promised that WRR would be her permanent home. She mentioned that this was a rather unusual animal but went into no details.

It was later that day when the young woman arrived with her bundle. She walked slowly up to the door, teary-eyed, carrying a large patchwork quilt that was undulating in her arms. Over her shoulder was a large canvas bag bulging with cat toys, treats, tiny flannel-covered pillows, and several bottles of mineral water. Suddenly, as she stepped inside the living room, out from a corner of the tattered quilt popped one tiny, pointed, precious, little head. But this was no ordinary head of an ordinary skunk; this little head had a decidedly pointed nose and just above it were two of the brightest pink eyes one could imagine, and this slick little head was also white as snow. We placed the quilt on the floor and out wriggled a chubby albino skunk. Her person began to explain that the obvious was what she was afraid to go into much detail about over the telephone. She was afraid that if I knew the skunk was an albino I might not have taken her in. I assured the young lady that it made no difference to me and that the snow-white skunk was indeed welcome to stay. This began a several-year relationship with the only albino skunk I have ever had the pleasure of knowing.

The female skunk had been given the name "Fiorella" which I was told meant "flower" in Italian. I was informed that she only drank mineral water, preferred flannel-covered pillows and sheets to plain cotton, and loved to play with her cat toys and, oh yes, was particularly fond of sweets and any high-calorie treats that I cared to offer little "Fiorella." I must tell you now that "Fiorella" was not really so little; to say that she was chubby is being quite kind. In fact her body mass was rapidly overtaking her short but sturdy little skunk legs. Someone was in need of a diet and I had a strong sense that this would be a totally new concept to our little "Snow White." But a diet was definitely in her future if she was to live as long as possible. It is not uncommon for albinos to have a shorter life span and I wanted to do everything I could to keep this "little one" healthy and content. There was no way I could know that she was one determined, headstrong skunk who had long ago made up her mind as to just how she would live her life—long, short, or somewhere in between.

The first clue she gave me was when I set up her sleeping quarters (complete with flannel-covered pillows and brightly-colored, flowered, flannel sheets) in one of the kitchen cabinets. Knowing that skunks are nocturnal, I assumed that she would like a cozy, dark den to spend her days in—somewhere she could be out of the way and have her space and privacy. Not quite. Her first action as the new self-appointed "Queen of the House" was to, article by article, methodically remove the carefully-placed bedding. She did this by fluffing up each sheet with her petite pink and white paws, and when it was just right, delicately baring her needle-sharp teeth, securing the linens in her mouth, and painstakingly dragging them across the kitchen floor, through the open doorway leading into the hall, down the hall, and into the bathroom to the laundry hamper. Once there, she pawed at the hamper door until it sprang open, then the clever little albino performed the same ritual on the laundry as she had on her sheets, removed it piece by piece and replaced the discarded clothes with her preferred flannel bedding. I watched in utter amazement as the chubby skunk went about the task of making my house her home. She was completely undisturbed by the fact that she was now sharing a house with two bobcats, a handful of juvenile raccoons, two injured adult opossums, and several small cages of birds. But I did notice that as she passed the room with the birds, she seemed to make a mental note to be sure to go back and check them out more closely; who knows, maybe they were part of that new diet she heard me mention. I realized that the new pleasingly-plump resident would have her way, so I might as well give in now and go shopping for a wicker basket because the laundry hamper was her new home.

As the months passed, the skunk formerly known as "Fiorella" (I simply called her White Skunk) became a cherished member of the WRR household. Though I believe she never really approved, she politely accepted her diet of mealworms, sweet potatoes, tomatoes, other fruits and vegetables, and some dry cat food, and slowly lost a pound or two. But all in all, she retained her rotund and comfortably round, baby-fat figure. White Skunk was a very agreeable sort; I would learn just how agreeable when the orphaned baby skunks began to come my way in need of intensive care and lots of mothering.

By the spring of the following year, the word had spread about Wildlife Rescue. Usually the description was more like, "There is this strange woman who lives with a bunch of wild animals on the north side of town." But people called nonetheless when there were animals in trouble and for those early days, that was the immediate goal. We had a rainy spring that year and for certain species of wildlife, heavy rains can be deadly for their young. Baby skunks are particularly vulnerable as they are sheltered deep inside the den and if rushing waters hit before mom has time to move them out, this can mean the end of their young lives. This drama seemed to play out time and time again that year. For well over two weeks, I was receiving litters of baby skunks. Sadly, many arrived dead or died within a few hours. They had all been found soaked, cold, and their little lungs were often gurgling from the water they had swallowed. There were those who did survive, but it was not because of my care; it was because of one motherly White Skunk who, though no one knew it, had a very caring heart beating inside her.

The first indication I had was one day when I was feeding a litter of babies. These tiny black and white-striped infants were crying; they wanted their mother and all I could do was offer them formula and a soft, warm bed. They continued to whine and weep until their cries were heard all the way into the laundry hamper in the bathroom. It was mid-morning and all the resident mammals were asleep, but these particular cries held special meaning for one snoozing skunk. The chubby girl could not sleep through the sad sound of her own kind. As she rounded the corner into the kitchen, her pink eyes barely open, White Skunk approached the cardboard box that cradled the crying orphans. She pawed at the box and before I could stop her, tipped it over, and began tugging at the soft bedding filled with helpless babies. I was afraid that she would see these infants as tasty morsels so I quickly scooped up the cloth and all the youngsters, or almost all. I placed the siblings into another box and began to prepare a new batch of formula. When I turned to pour the mixture into the tiny bottles, I noticed something dark on the floor under White Skunk. Had she brought a snack with her into the kitchen? No, there was no snack, but there was a tiny baby who might soon become one! I grabbed for the infant and was met with a sharp bite to my hand. There would be none of that; someone had other plans for this baby. In only moments the cries of the baby skunk stopped; he had no more reasons to cry, for he was being loved by his new mother. He did not notice or care that she was an albino; all he knew was that he was being lovingly licked, cleaned, and gently tucked into her soft, warm, snow-white fur. There the two sat on the kitchen floor, this dear albino girl and her newly adopted infant. And there I sat with three boxes full of screaming skunk babies. Suddenly things did not look so bad. I was not sure how we would do it but I knew we could work something out.

I fed the remaining babies then placed their boxes on the floor. The chubby girl made her way into the boxes, and one-by-one sniffed, licked, and comforted each tiny motherless skunk. She then waddled off back to her home in the hamper. I was thankful that the new arrivals had been comforted by her and knew this would help ensure their survival. I arranged the babies' boxes on the heating pads and went about the tasks of caring for the other animals in the house. No more than an hour passed before I returned to the "skunk nursery" but something was very different. All the babies had disappeared; the bedding was in place but not a baby was in sight. I hoped I had not made a terrible mistake and misinterpreted White Skunk's motives. I was reluctant, to say the least, but I had to find out what had happened. As I walked toward the bathroom I heard the cries of the infant skunks. Were they being eaten after all? This did not sound good. I hated to look, but there were no other options. I pulled the hamper door open ever so slowly. Some of the flannel bedding had fallen out onto the floor, but there was no sign of any babies. I looked to the very back of the deep cabinet and there, in the midst of the flowered sheets, was one snow-white, self-appointed mother skunk, her bright-pink eyes seeming to shine in the dark, her round, soft body covered with her contented, sleeping, newly-adopted black and white babies. There was no mistaking her motives. The albino skunk, who had been taken from *her* mother so that she could be sold as a "pet," had heard the cries of other babies who also had lost their mothers, and she, then and there, decided to create a family of her own.

For the next several weeks as I continued to feed the infant skunks, White Skunk continued to care for them in the way only a mother could. As they grew, she shared her mealworms with them, taught them how to be independent, tolerated them as they became adolescents, and when the day came for them to be set free, she seemed to make her peace with the natural process of letting go. This remarkable snow-white beauty carried out this service for over five years. As she grew older, she was less able to help but every time new baby skunks came to WRR, she was there watching over them, comforting them, making their life in our care more tolerable, until one sad day she left us.

It was a cold, rainy, winter morning when I found her round, lifeless body sound "asleep" in her laundry hamper home. She had quietly and so peacefully died during the night. This wonderful gentle being never knew the life of a truly free and wild skunk, but she was never without the company of her own kind. She had made her home at Wildlife Rescue when I had nothing to offer her but a cozy spot in her chosen hamper. But what she gave to me and to dozens of motherless babies will always be treasured in these bittersweet memories of those days twenty-nine years ago, that now, thinking of her, make it seem like only yesterday.

Skunks Welcomed Here

It was about the fourth call Wildlife Rescue had received regarding a skunk in trouble. The year was 1977, early summer, and people were just discovering that there was a new organization in San Antonio that was willing to rescue this much-maligned mammal. The first few calls asked us to rescue skunks who had yogurt containers stuck on their heads, but this call was considerably more involved than that. It seems that there was a mother skunk who had dug her den under a sidewalk near the Riverwalk in downtown San Antonio. She could not have chosen a busier site. Because it was near such a popular nightspot and because skunks are nocturnal, we had the perfect recipe for chaos. We contacted the city public works office, asked them to meet us just after sunset, and hoped for the best. The restaurant owners in the area wanted the mother skunk killed. We explained that not only was that not acceptable, but there were babies under that sidewalk who would starve to death without their mom. Saving a protective mother skunk who is inclined to spray at the approach of anyone threatening her young was not going to be easy. Getting to the babies under that horizontal wall of concrete was also going to present some challenges. The owners of the restaurants agreed to give us two days to "get the family out of there."

The first task was to capture mom. We set a live trap and waited. It was only minutes after midnight when she agreed to take the bait and go into the trap. Now we were at least a third of the way home. There was no way of knowing how many babies were under the sidewalk, but the public works officials kindly offered to dig as deep as necessary to reach the youngsters. It looked as if this was not going to be so difficult after all. Of course, looks can sometimes be deceiving.

The excavating had just begun when over the two-way radio came an emergency call; all public works trucks were needed to repair several water lines that had burst on the far northeast side of town. Suddenly our wonderful rescue crew and all of their "we cannot possibly do this without it" equipment was driving off into the night.

Now there were just the three of us: a very unhappy trapped mother skunk, a volunteer, and me with only one shovel. It was time to start digging. Cement is the perfect substance for sidewalks. I imagine it is also, from a skunk's perspective, the perfect place under which to birth babies, but to retrieve those babies from beneath it is no picnic. We were forty-five minutes into the task and already feeling hopeless. Apparently we looked as hopeless as we felt because some kind soul took it upon himself to contact the news media. Two a.m. can be a slow time for good stories, so one radio and two television stations decided to come downtown and see what Wildlife Rescue was up to. The television stations were happy to air the story the next day, but we needed help that moment. The reporter from the radio station moved into action, and suddenly the plight of the skunk family was broadcast all over San Antonio. In less than an hour we had more people, picks, shovels, and skunk-lovers than we could have hoped for. Just before daybreak, because of the help of twelve good people, we had four tiny, blind, black and white baby skunks in our hands. After placing the babies on a clean, soft towel we reunited them with their anxious mother still pacing in the trap. We decided to hold them overnight, to give mom time to realize that when she vacated the trap she needed to remember to take her kids (as if she needed our help to remember that small detail). That same evening after mom had dined on a hearty meal of bananas, grapes, and dry cat food, the skunk babies curled up close to their mother's tummy, nursed for about twenty minutes, and fell fast asleep. They had all survived a very traumatic experience.

The following night it was time to send the mother skunk and her babies back to their life in the wild. Since they were so accustomed to living in an urban setting, we did not want to take them too far away. Urban wildlife have made their home alongside us, and it is in their best interest to let them remain in an urban setting. We were fortunate that one of the gentlemen who volunteered to help us excavate the babies had a two-acre fenced yard about five miles from downtown San Antonio. He was happy to have the skunk family relocated to his property. At approximately ten o'clock at night, Momma Skunk and her four babies were given their freedom in their new home. The area was secluded, quiet, and safe; there were plenty of trees and two out-buildings; Momma Skunk could choose her favorite spot. As she emerged from the trap, her tail erect, her nose to the ground, mom was on her way. She stopped about ten feet from the trap, looked around, and spied the wooden shed. Momma Skunk had found her new home. One by one, she gently collected her babies in her tiny mouth, carried them to the shed, dug just the right-sized entrance hole, and disappeared only to reemerge and gather up one more baby. In only minutes the family was tucked safely away in their new den.

Because of some very compassionate people, what could have been a tragedy was instead a complete success. Together we not only saved a family, but we learned a valuable lesson. When you least expect it, there are many people in the world who feel as you do about animals. And, perhaps in a show of gratitude, the mother skunk never even sprayed.

Dove Love

I'm not sure that I understand why it is, but I have always noticed that we humans find it easy to rank other beings in order of their perceived importance. I remember in the early days of WRR, I was often asked if we were going to "even rescue pigeons?" I always thought this was an odd question, but as the years passed, I often heard that others who were carrying out similar work of rescuing and rehabilitating animals in need, would simply kill pigeons instead of investing any time or resources to save them. Clearly the "lowly pigeon" was one of those beings many had decided to categorize as unworthy.

As is often the case when you've had the opportunity to get to know someone, whether they be human or non-human, your perception of who they are can change drastically. Pigeons have always been interesting to me. They are stout of body and able to live in the concrete domains that we so readily create and call cities. I have always wondered how they are able to survive and raise their vulnerable young on skyscraper ledges and the most dangerous of all nooks, the undersides of the massive bridges that stretch over our deadly freeways.

It is here that the story of Pidge begins. Impossible as it may seem, Pidge survived one of the most nearly fatal accidents you and I could ever imagine. Early one weekday morning years ago, during a pouring rain, a gentleman was driving from his home on the outskirts of town to his job in San Antonio. As he passed under an overpass, something plopped onto the hood of his car. He assumed it was mud or leaves or something being tossed up by a passing motorist. The rain was hitting so hard it never occurred to him to stop. So on he went through the rain in the traffic making his way to the city. When he finally came to a stop, it was so late that he simply hurried out of his vehicle and into his office. It was not until the end of the day that he remembered the sound of something hitting his car and thought to take a look before making his way back home. When he did, he was not sure what he was looking at. There on the hard metal hood of his car sat a cold, soaking wet lump of gray and dark blue feathers. When he approached the lump, suddenly out of nowhere popped a beak and the tiniest of voices cheeping for food.

The driver was amazed. Had this baby simply dropped out of the sky, or could this have been the thud he heard as he passed under the overpass? When he arrived at WRR with the exhausted bundle, a quick examination of the nestling's underside told the story. The bruising was massive and every time you touched the baby on his breast, he would squirm and cry. One of the little one's legs was badly broken. During the early morning rush hour as the gentleman passed under the overpass, something had happened in the pigeon's nest. This baby fell at just the right time to hit the hood of a car instead of the pavement where he would have been killed immediately by another car. Now he was safe at WRR and though his injuries were serious, we felt certain that we could save him.

After we applied a splint to his tiny leg and filled his crop with some warm nourishing formula, the little bird tried to get into a comfortable position. He squirmed and wiggled, and finally while leaning hard to the left, he fell fast asleep. WRR had not taken in any other pigeons when this nestling was brought to us; it was sad to see him all alone, and to listen to his cheeps that no one would answer. But it was spring and we were rescuing mockingbirds, cardinals, sparrows, and one rather elderly white-winged dove. This dove had been brought to WRR after being found in a backyard in San Antonio. She was thin and lethargic and would not fly away when approached even though her wings were in fine shape. She was very old and seemed just to be accepting the fact that her life was nearing its end.

At that time, our makeshift nursery had only used carriers and sturdy cardboard boxes in which to house our patients. The birds who were too young to fly seemed comfortable in their warm boxes, and the others remained in carriers until they were well enough to go out of doors into larger areas. The elderly dove did not fit into any of these categories as she could only slightly flutter, and she seemed quite content strolling about the floor of the nursery. There she would regularly visit her platter of fresh seeds, scatter them about, dine on her share, and then wander over to the small low-lying branch in the corner of the room. This was her routine day after day. She showed no interest in any other activity. Not, that is, until the day that Pidge arrived.

Elderly Dove was never very impressed by the baby birds we rescued. She would listen to their calls, show a slight curiosity during their many feedings throughout the day, and then go about her business of patrolling the wide expanse of floor. But the day Pidge arrived, all of that would change. Every time we would feed Pidge, he would flutter his short, strong wings, cheep and cheep at the top of his little lungs, and all but inhale his formula. And every time this ritual was carried out, Elderly Dove would sit attentively nearby and watch and listen to all the commotion going on in the big cardboard box. As the days passed, Elderly Dove ceased her patrolling of the nursery floor. She wanted only to sit beneath the box that held the coos of the baby pigeon. We talked about allowing her into the box with the growing youngster, but he was so rambunctious and she so frail that we were concerned for her safety. But as usual, animals know best and early one morning as we were preparing to begin the daunting task of feeding dozens of hungry baby birds, we noticed someone was missing. We searched the floor, every corner and under every table, but Elderly Dove was nowhere to be found.

The other noticeable element that was missing was the cheeping from the largest box in the room—the box that held Pidge. Our attention focused on the quiet box and we feared the very worst had happened overnight. Apprehensively, we peered over the edge of the deep box—there was Pidge sleeping quietly and there by his bruised and aching side was Elderly Dove. Somehow during the night she had mustered the strength to flutter her way up and into the company of the lonely little pigeon. Here slept the two of them quiet and warm. Since she was so old and so frail and since this youngster was not her own, I did not expect Elderly Dove to produce any "milk" in her crop as she would readily have done for her own chicks. But once again, we humans knew little about how far one animal will go for another, even one who is not a relative and is not one of their own species. By noon that same day, Pidge could not have been happier. Elderly Dove was feeding him, cooing over him, keeping him warm, and being the very best mom she could be. She too seemed to be more content and at ease. She never left their box to go patrolling the floor; she wanted only to be by the side of her new baby.

As the weeks passed, Pidge grew into a huge and gorgeous bird. His scraggly feathers were now full and smooth and the most beautiful slate gray mingled with dark hues of blue and charcoal. He dwarfed Elderly Dove but nonetheless, she was still his mom. We moved them into a large wooden cage and in no time, the dove had her adopted youngster perching and eating seed from a bowl. I knew the time was drawing near when we would have to separate the two. Pidge was ready to go free and take his place amongst the other pigeons who flew free on the sanctuary grounds. We were all worried how this would affect Elderly Dove. Once again she would be alone in the world. But Pidge was strong and ready to go and it was only fair to set him free.

It was a beautiful summer morning, and the time seemed perfect to open the door of the cage and let the once bruised and broken Pidge take to the sky. The plan was to take Elderly Dove back into the nursery and let her resume her life as the resident matriarch. But it seemed that she had other plans. As we opened the door to the cage there was much fluttering and excitement. But all the anticipation was coming only from Pidge. There in the soft hay was the beautiful female dove. She had passed away in the night and there, fluttering by her side, was her baby. Pidge knew something was very wrong that sad morning. His mother did not stir and no matter how he coaxed and cooed, she would not move. He had lost his gentle Elderly Dove who could not resist his cheeps all those weeks ago. She had rescued him when he needed her most; she had found the strength to give her all one more time as she had done, no doubt, countless times in the wild to her own babies. Now he was alone, and he could no longer lean on her for comfort or for strength.

But for Pidge there was a new life waiting. He peered curiously out of the cage door and saw high above, the flock of pigeons winging about the oaks. He tilted his head as he heard their calls. These were not the calls of his now dead mother, but they were familiar nonetheless. They were the calls of his own kind. It was time for Pidge to reclaim his life and he did just that. His flight was steady and sure as he leapt from the confines of the cage. In a moment he was one of the flock, flying and circling, accepted as if he had hatched among them. This once tiny bird whose fall was almost fatal, had instead been taken in by a kind old dove who had given him her very best, and who now would live on only in his memories.

Oreo Finds A Mother

For years now, WRR has on occasion rescued chickens, ducks, geese, and other animals commonly found on farms. One of the very first such animals we rescued was a sad mother black-faced ewe. Suffolk sheep have the most wonderful faces that go with their rotund, off-white, wool-covered bodies. Their faces are solid black, matching their equally ebony hooves. This particular female was quite large and quite old. She had been used as a "breeder sheep" producing lambs who were always fat and beautiful and healthy, but now that she had grown old this would no longer be possible for her. Three days after the lamb who would be her last baby was born, it was clear that her life would never be the same.

The tiny, black-faced lamb was small but looked healthy enough just hours after he was born. He stood and wobbled and fell but got up again and stood strong and steady as he nudged his mother's belly looking for the first sign of a meal. He suckled for several minutes then dropped into the bed of hay next to his mother and fell asleep. This ritual was repeated hour after hour for the first twenty-four hours of his life. By day two, the newborn ram was only interested in eating once or twice in the morning. By midday he wanted only to sleep safe and comfortable next to his proud mother. There is no doubt that Mother Sheep knew something was not right, but she never let on. She cleaned her baby, licked his tiny, black mouth, kept him warm, and never left his side to go out into the pasture with the other sheep. She was devoted and loving; it did not matter to her that all of her knowledge as an experienced mother kept telling her that something was terribly wrong with her little one. Well after midnight on the third day of the young ram's life the chances for his survival rapidly diminished. Before daybreak he began to cry out for his mother; he wanted to stand but could not. He had grown cold overnight and was shivering as he lay in the warm hay. Mother Sheep licked and cleaned and nudged at her baby; she called to him, letting him know she was near. Staying close, she watched as he grew weaker; she listened as his cries became audible only to her ears.

When her people came to check on the ewe and her new lamb, their eyes were met with this sad scene: an old momma sheep, her last baby dying by her side, and she trying her best to care for the infant who was so quickly slipping away from her. For all of these years, all they had thought of was what a wonderful "breeder" this female sheep had been; all they cared about was the lambs she would provide for their stock but now they realized that for all of these years something much more had been going on before their eyes, something they had watched but never *seen*.

They stayed with the two sheep; they sat as the mother licked her now cold, dead baby; they cried as she nudged his soft, black muzzle hoping he would respond, stand, and once again probe her belly for dinner. But there was no response from the infant; he had slipped away from her even as she stood over him. Even as he lay beside her, somehow he had slipped away.

It was mid-morning before they could take the baby away to bury him in a nearby field. As they did, so Mother Sheep watched; she never took her eyes off of them. She followed at a distance and saw exactly where they put her baby and it was there that they would find her every morning, every night—there where her last baby was buried. This went on for days until everyone watching knew something had to be done.

When the call came in to WRR, we were not certain that we could help. The old sheep, it seemed, had lost her desire to live. But perhaps a change of scenery and a tiny, orphaned goat could help. We instructed the farmers to bring the elderly ewe to the sanctuary in Boerne and we would all try our best and keep our fingers crossed that our plan would work. We were not just thinking of the sheep, for we also had a "problem child" to consider.

A week or so before the sheep call we had been asked to take in a baby goat; he was one of twins. His mother had rejected him for she barely had enough milk for one baby. We were doing everything in our power to interest this orphan in a bottle of formula, and we were failing miserably.

It was late on a Tuesday afternoon when the despondent ewe arrived. Her beautiful black head drooped from her once strong shoulders; her eyes showed no sign of interest in her new surroundings. We led her into a fenced area where there was lush green grass, a three-sided wooden shelter, and a tall oak tree offering itself as shade for the old sheep with the sad face. The old girl walked about the pasture, munched on some small sprigs of grass, made her way to the shelter, and plopped down depressed into the waiting bed of hay and alfalfa. It seemed that she was ready to give up but little did she know that only yards away was a thin, but determined, little guy who had other plans for her future. The only question was: Do we wait to introduce the two or do we throw caution to the wind and move forward with our plan? As is usually the case, the non-human animals have plans of their own, and this time was no exception. The baby goat was coal black except for a large splash of white over his left eye and a few matching dots on his cute little rump. Everyone at WRR lovingly called him Oreo. Since he was a domestic animal we all agreed it was all right to bestow a name on the little ram. Oreo was bedded down in a big carrier just the other side of the fence that separated him from the old girl sheep. His appetite was not great but his shiny, black nose was working just fine because in no time he began to sniff the air. His stub of a tail twitched and his curiosity led him out of his carrier and directly to the wire fence. Oreo's small head poked through an opening in the mesh barrier; he pushed and strained and in minutes had managed to squeeze his frail frame through to the other side. The spring grass was almost as tall as Oreo; it brushed his belly and swallowed up his short legs, but it did not keep him from his goal. Something told him there was a mother hiding in that pasture and he was going to find her.

We watched as little Oreo stumbled through the field; what we knew to be only several yards must have seemed like miles to his thin body. He cried out. It was to us a sad and desperate cry, but to the longing ears of a lonely mother sheep it was an all too familiar cry for help. Mother Sheep baaaed back. Did she think this was her lost lamb, even after she witnessed his burial. Had she somehow found him again? It did not seem to matter. Oreo cried out even louder now, he knew she was there; somewhere in that tall grass he knew she was waiting. He could smell her, and now he could even hear her. Mother Sheep called out again and this time she could see who had been calling to her. Would it matter to her that this was not her baby?

Oreo ran as best he could to the old sheep; he immediately began butting his tiny head into her soft stomach. Old Sheep moved away. She pushed Oreo with her big, black head, and he fell into the tall grass. This was not her lost lamb; she now knew this was not her baby. Oreo stood up, stumbled after the sheep and tried again, and again she rejected him. She walked back to her shelter and now looked more alone than ever. Old Sheep lay down in the hay. Oreo found his way to her side and there he stood looking at this mother who did not act like a mother, this mother who had milk but not for him. Our plan had failed. We would have to try again with a bottle of formula for little Oreo and hope that time would help the sheep.

We decided to leave them together; at least they had each other's company. Hours passed; Oreo would not take our bottle, and we once again had to resort to feeding him with a stomach tube. He cried out and struggled; he hated this method of feeding more than we hated having to inflict it on him. The warm formula began to fill his stomach but quickly Oreo pulled away and as he did he yanked the tube out of his mouth. The milk squirted all over his face and again he cried out in frustration. He was hungry and no one seemed to be able to give him what he wanted. Oreo stood there crying, his face covered with milk. We reached for a towel that was sitting on top of the shelter and as we turned back to Oreo there was Mother Sheep doing our job for us. The once sad mother saw a baby with a dirty face, heard him crying to be fed, and could not resist. Oreo's tail was wagging in sheer delight and now Mother Sheep was once again caring for a baby. It did not matter that he had not been her baby, for now, as far as she was concerned, Oreo was her little lamb.

Mother Takes Another

When working with non-human animals, there is always the element of unpredictability. This is especially true when working with wild animals. One learns very quickly that these incredibly intelligent, sensitive creatures have more depth of feeling and emotion than the human community ever dares to give them credit for. For those who are fortunate enough to be in the company of these animals and wise enough to step back, watch, learn, and appreciate, there will be many opportunities to witness these attributes.

Perhaps one of the saddest sights we are faced with in wildlife rehabilitation is that of a baby wild animal who has lost her mother. The babies who are old enough to realize their loss and who continue to either cry out for or search for their mother are surely some of the most tragic. It was not so very long ago that one of these babies found her way to Wildlife Rescue. There have been more than we could ever count over the past many years—mostly raccoons, skunks, opossums, squirrels, birds, and foxes; but there have also been the bobcat kittens.

This little one was not so different from the others. Her mother had been hit and killed on one of our highways. She was sitting there cuddled up by her dead mother's body. She was young, still nursing, still totally dependent on mom, but she was old enough to realize what had happened to her, old enough to know that her life had, in an instant, forever changed. A compassionate passerby found her, took pity on her, and brought her to the sanctuary. She was terrified, hungry, and wanting no one but her mother. There is nothing we can offer but food and shelter at these times. Wild animals do not take comfort in our intended soothing words the way a dog or cat would; they do not look to us for help; we are simply the feared enemy, the ones who prey upon them, the ones who, for countless generations, they have been taught to avoid at all costs. And now here she was in our hands with no mother to protect her, no mother to comfort her, no mother to feed and shelter her. We did our best to provide her with the formula necessary to keep her body and soul together. She calmed enough to nurse from a bottle, but fortunately she remained wild, needing our care but never really wanting it.

Shortly before we took in this little one, we had been called upon to rescue a mother bobcat with kittens. The mother's leg had been mutilated when she was caught in a steel jaw leghold trap. She had made her way into a burned-out barn, and was found hiding, one of her tiny infant kittens already dead. She was thin and in need of medical attention. Her rescuers called on Texas Parks and Wildlife and they called on WRR for help.

We did our best to keep our distance while providing the care she needed so that she could take better care of her baby. Both were in poor condition and both wanted only to be left alone. As the mother grew stronger, so did the kitten. They did not have much of a life compared to being free but they were showing signs of making a full recovery. The weeks passed and we felt certain that both would survive. During this time, our single bobcat kitten was living a life of solitude. She too was growing stronger and was remembering her short life in the wild in the care of her mother.

Finally the day came to place the mother and baby outside in one of our rehabilitation enclosures. In only moments they were enjoying the fresh air and quiet of life under a stand of oak trees. Here at least they could hide up in the sleeping boxes and the kitten could play among the tree limbs. Suddenly life was a little less stressful. But this was not the case for our single female kitten. She too wanted to be out of doors, she too wanted to play, but for her there were no playmates. It was time to make a decision for her future.

We knew that even though the two bobcat kittens were not precisely the same age, they were about the same size and we were counting on their playfulness to override any threat they would be to each other. But what about the mother bobcat? She was another story. If she decided she did not want the orphan then it could mean death to the little female. The enclosure allowed everyone her own space to hide in, but a disapproving mother bobcat would be impossible to avoid. We placed the orphan in a carrier in the enclosure. In less than thirty minutes the mother's kitten was down on the ground investigating this new addition to his world. He pawed gently at the carrier door and from inside, the little female slapped back at him. She growled and decided it was time to look and act very tough and very brave. Then just as quickly the little male would dart off, bounding about the enclosure, jumping from limb to limb playing with all of the kitten energy he could muster. For the little female life was not so simple. She sat looking sad and curious. Her world had not so long ago included a loving mother. For too long there had not been any warm fur to nuzzle in, no one near to protect her. Now for the first time in months was an opportunity to play, here out of nowhere was another bobcat in her world. Her tiny round paw reached out every time the male kitten came near. She was not so interested in slapping anymore; maybe if she was quiet he would stay and keep her company. This ritual of run and slap and growl and hop went on for an entire day. By nightfall both kittens were exhausted. The male went up to sleep comfortably with his mother; the single little female curled up alone in the back of her carrier just as she had done for so many nights before.

By the third day, the ritual had grown stale. The young male was holding back on his invitations to play, the young female was tired of her confinement. Even though there was still the very real fact of the mother to consider, it was time to make a change. We decided that early morning was best; this way we could observe during the day, and if things did not go well we would perhaps have some way of saving the baby's life. We opened the carrier, and the little lone female walked to the edge of the door. She stood there surveying her new surroundings, looking more than a little nervous about what to expect. From his vantage point on high, next to his mother, the young male looked down. Things looked very different indeed now that his new playmate was accessible. He bounded down through the limbs, down to the ground to confront the interloper. Short, quick tails began twitching, fur bristled, growls were exchanged, slaps were traded, no doubt questions that we will never understand were being asked. But youth has its advantages. There was no real fear, no real anger, just the curiosity of innocence. And that wonderful curiosity turned to play in only minutes. First the little female, so glad to be free to run, took advantage of every limb, every vertical space to climb and explore. Then the male joined in, chasing, unearthing little rocks and twigs with his exuberance. The two had found each other. Each kitten now had a sibling.

The mother bobcat was not so comfortable with this new arrangement. We could see just how cautious she was. Shortly before dusk, the male kitten decided it was time to cuddle up with mom. The little female stood quietly as her newfound friend climbed up the limbs to his mother; she stood on the ground just staring up to that tree limb. Suddenly she was alone again. After a perfect day of play and companionship, she found herself once again on her own. She turned, looked about for a place to rest and walked back into her carrier. Because we could not stand watch overnight, we decided to close the door, and as we did, her round little paw reached out, scraped the ground, and then quietly drew back.

The following morning we decided to get an early start on the introduction. Her carrier door was opened and out bounded the playful female. But this morning something had changed. The little male did not run to meet her; he was not moving from his mother's side. No matter, the female seemed to decide. She had played alone before and she could continue to do so if she had to. I suspect it was this very determination that was a factor in creating what happened next. When the little kitten's back was turned, the mother bobcat crept ever so quietly down the oak limbs. We watched not wanting to interfere but afraid for the worst. If the mother wanted to, she could easily kill the kitten. There is no way we can know what was in the mother's mind as she approached the little female; we can only interpret what we saw. The kitten was slapping at a leaf-covered twig, and as it would respond to her slaps she would hit it again, making it move and come to life enough to respond to her. She stopped for one very still moment as the mother approached, no doubt understanding the potential danger of the situation. She did not turn, she did not acknowledge the mother's presence; she only stopped momentarily then went about her game of "slap the twig." The mother bobcat sniffed her and batted her gently on her small fuzzy rump. The baby ignored her. The mother cat growled and moved to the kitten's side; the little girl turned her head away from the approaching adult. The bobcat kitten took a few cautious steps away and continued her preoccupation with her surroundings, finding bits of rock to turn or an insect to sniff. The mother bobcat moved closer, reached out her huge paw and hit the baby once again on her rump. The wise kitten pretended she was not there. Now the mother cat appeared to grow impatient. She uttered a low growl-meow, reached out her paw, caught the kitten's rear leg and pulled her back. Our first reaction was to run in, chase the mother away and stop what was about to happen, but we could not move as fast as a bobcat. We humans are not only slow to move—we are also slow to grasp communication between non-human animals. In less than a moment, the mother bobcat had the little female kitten under her; the kitten growled but the mother would not listen. She began licking the baby, purring over the tiny, furred body. The lone kitten returned her purrs, slapped gently at the old female's face, twitched her bobbed tail, and seemed to melt in the care of her brand new mother. The two carried on for several minutes, then the mother bobcat called the young male to join them. The three were now a family. After living through more loss and tragedy than most of us could bear, these three had managed to survive it all, find each other, and create a new life. Soon, as a family, the three will be set free. They will once again have the chance to live life on their terms, in the wild that each of them no doubt remembers well.

They Saved Each Other's Lives

Every year we have an abundance of incoming orphaned, injured, and sick baby wild animals. Just as predictable, every year we rescue a greater number of one particular species. We found the last year of the century to be the year of the opossum.

Looking over the carriers, boxes, and nursery cages containing the dark, yet bright-eyed, softly-furred bodies, I remember the literally thousands of these incredible marsupials who we have seen through the years. They have come to us after suffering the trauma of being slammed by a swiftly moving automobile, chewed to a near-death condition by an overly excited dog, clubbed by teenage boys, and poisoned with deadly toxins, yet miraculously, time and time again they would survive.

This was not due so much to our heroic efforts to save their lives as it was to the opossum's ability to survive life-threatening events. These animals are unique in that they have a slower metabolic rate and, consequently, a lower than average body temperature and a slower heart rate. Apparently these factors contribute to their innate ability to survive almost anything. Interestingly, the opossum can endure emotional loss as well, but with this sometimes they need a little help, not just anyone's help, but help of just the right kind.

It has been over six years since the mother opossum came to us, all of her babies dead. She had been found on the side of a road late one night, her pouch filled with tiny babies. All had been victims of a collision with a car. Baby opossums were strewn about the road, Mom was lying bloody and broken. Quietly, the car moved on into the night. Left behind to slowly die, she was seen some time later by a passing motorist. The possum family was gathered up, placed in a box, and brought to the sanctuary.

By the time they arrived, the babies were dead, all thirteen of them. Momma Possum was barely hanging onto life. Several hours later, after intense fluid therapy, Momma Possum was standing, trying to walk, and sniffing about the carrier looking for her babies. When no young were found she began to investigate her pouch, licking, probing, and once again finding no one. In only a matter of days, Momma Opossum was beginning to feed herself. She would take small bites of fresh, raw chicken and slices of purple grapes. She seemed interested, but soon we were to realize that she was not eating enough to keep body and soul together.

As the days passed, the mother with no babies began to show distinct signs of depression. Her appetite plummeted; she would sleep both day and night. She spent little or no time investigating her living quarters. Day by day, she was deciding to die. We moved her to a larger outside area. Fresh-cut tree limbs and a soft bed of fragrant, green alfalfa would hopefully bring back her interest in eating and maybe restore her will to live.

Another week passed and Momma Opossum was not improving. Once again, fluid therapy was necessary. Once again, she was at death's door. Two days later she rallied. She was lapping a special formula, walking about, and renewing our hope for her future. This time we were taking no chances.

We placed a young, attractive male opossum in her carrier. Perhaps the companionship would be just what she needed. We were sadly mistaken. *He* was interested in the new relationship, but Momma Opossum did not share his enthusiasm. The young male was ready to be released, so we gave him his freedom and tried another male who had been rescued from the jaws of a large dog. Maybe their shared traumatic past would make them a more compatible pair. Wrong once more! Momma Opossum was not interested. She was still not willing to eat, socialize, or get back to the business of living. Now, we were faced with the dilemma: Do we let her quietly drift off or do we continue to harass and stress her with IV fluids, forced feedings, and maybe save her life?

Very early one morning, a young woman called WRR. She had just found a small opossum in her backyard. He was lethargic and covered with fleas. She was instructed to bring him to the sanctuary immediately. When he arrived, we saw that he was anemic, had a severe infection in his right eye, and his fur was matted and dry. After removing all of the fleas, treating his eye, and tube-feeding him, he was placed on a heating pad in a small, cardboard box. Inadvertently, we had placed the young, sick opossum right next to the grieving Mom.

An hour later when we went to check on the new patient we were met with sounds of scratching and sniffing. But, these welcomed sounds were not coming from the weak male, they were coming from the carrier just next to his. Momma Opossum had suddenly come back to life. She was frantic to get to the little male just outside her carrier door. We knew his chances for survival were not good, but maybe Momma Opossum could help him. And by helping him, could help herself.

We placed the two in a large, hay-filled cage. There was a bowl of sliced bananas, apples, and grapes. Beside that, was a small bowl of fresh water. One wooden sleeping box was furnished for privacy. The Momma Opossum wasted no time. She deliberately walked over to the weak youngster, began licking his injured eye, and in her best mothering behavior, had his dry, matted fur clean and fluffy in no time.

In the days to follow, Mom and her new baby grew to be an inseparable twosome. The young male never regained sight in his right eye, but by the time they were ready to live in an outdoor enclosure, Momma Opossum was willing and able to look after him whenever he needed her. Climbing on the thick oak limbs, the male would often lose his footing, but Mom was always there to coax him back up to the top of the cage and encourage him to try once more. This incredible once near-lifeless mother opossum who had lost everything, even her will to live, had found someone who could not survive without her. A young opossum who, without even trying, had brought her back to life and given her a reason to live.

It was well after midnight on the evening that mother and now half-grown baby were set free. A gentle rain had fallen throughout the night and a warm breeze made its way over each branch of the stately, green cypress trees. The male was first to leave the confines of the carrier. His now single-vision perspective was no longer a challenge. He had long ago learned to compensate for his loss. As he made his way agilely through the tall, soft grass, his adopted mother was close behind. Together they climbed the angular branches of a bent oak. As they reached the top of the leafy canopy, the young male stopped to sniff the fresh, night air. Mom stopped too. Once again her soft, pink tongue caressed his scarred face. In only minutes, the two disappeared into the dark green mass.

Now their life was their own. They could stay together or go their separate ways, but whatever they decided, they had a bond from the experience of one incredible animal looking after another—two opossums who had courted death, but with the help of one another, had chosen life.

Taken In His Prime . . . Almost

All too often, we rescue birds whose only future is to live the remainder of their lives grounded. There is no way we can know what this is like for a bird—to never fly again, to never carry out his beautiful, most simply natural way of moving through this world. Perhaps it is easier to imagine what it is like for those hawks, owls, sparrows, cardinals, and mockingbirds who come through our doors sick, injured, temporarily grounded, to finally fully recover, to spread their wings and without hesitation, once again take to the open, endless sky.

When you have the privilege of working in the company of non-human animals everyday, you are often given the great gift of watching a raccoon, squirrel, turtle, or hawk fight to hold on to life, struggle against incredible odds to win the battle, and return to the wild. Some struggles seem more valiant, some less hopeful, some absolutely miraculous. I often wonder how it is that there are any wild animals left roaming this earth, after all of the brutal attempts mankind has made to destroy them.

One hawk in particular comes to mind. About four years ago, a young man drove up to the sanctuary gates, unloaded a huge cardboard box, and let himself in the front door. His pants were covered in dirt and vines up to the knees, there were scratches on his arms and face and his hair was a mess. He sat the box down on the floor and while dropping to his knees to open the box, began to tell us his story. He had been on a camping trip in a state park; he had only been there two days when he began hearing gunshots off in the distance. He contacted a game warden and expressed his concern, but no one seemed able to find the origin of the shots so there was little that could be done. On the fourth day of his trip he was hiking on a trail; once again he heard the shots and something high up in the sky caught his attention. There in the mid-morning, cloudy, light blue sky, he saw a red-tailed hawk soaring, dipping, and diving in sheer pleasure. He stopped to watch the sight, enjoying each moment until like a slap, a shot rang out, the huge bird swooned, flapped helplessly, then dropped, wings flailing in the air, down somewhere to the brush-covered earth. The young man was horrified; he knew he had to do something. If there was any chance that the hawk was alive, he had to at least try to find him. He spent the next three and a half hours climbing over rocks, scouring the hillside looking for the fallen bird. It was only moments after he had decided it was hopeless that he found the injured hawk.

The bird could not stand; there was blood in his left eye, his right leg hung weak and broken. Whoever had tried to mercilessly kill this bird had almost succeeded. But it was clear to the young man that this red-tailed hawk was not ready to give up the fight.

The young man left us a twenty-dollar bill and asked if he could call back and check on the hawk. We knew that we had our work cut out for us if we were going to have even a fighting chance to save this animal, but the real work was up to the bird. He was scared, in pain, and wanted no part of what we had to offer. His leg had to be splinted, there were tips of primary feathers that had been torn, and one eye was bloody and swollen. The positive side to all of this was that he was a young, healthy bird in good condition, and he had an incredible spirit; he made it quite clear that he was not going to sit quietly by and have his life literally shot out from under him.

During the first two weeks of care, the red-tailed hawk was feisty; he had to be force-fed, he screeched and threatened every time we came near. By the third week, his condition had deteriorated; he was losing weight, he was under constant stress, his eye was still puffy and his spirit was waning. We had to give his leg time to heal or he would have no chance of surviving in the wild. We felt certain that he had partial sight in the injured eye, but was it enough to enable him to seek out and catch his prey? A predatory bird must have sharp, accurate senses if he is going to survive in the wild. What this hawk needed now was a body that was as strong as his will.

The moment we removed the splint we could see the once limp and broken leg was solid and strong. The hawk gently tested the leg; he slowly moved about, cautiously, watching our intruding, hopeful eyes. Now our hope was renewed. If he would eat on his own, if he would once again tear at his food as he had in the wild, maybe, just maybe, he was on the road to recovery.

The next two weeks would tell us everything we needed to know. Once he was in a larger outdoor enclosure, the determined hawk seemed to make up his mind about his future. He spent his days at the highest perch he could find; he flapped his wings, he landed on the tree branches with certainty and grace. He never failed to hit his mark. He ate reluctantly, but finally he took the initiative to feed himself. We were no longer a necessary evil in his life. It was time to send him back, to once again let him take to the sky.

The morning we set him free was one of those cool, breezy autumn days. The leaves had begun to drop from their branches; the sun was not as bright as it was the day the red-tailed hawk had been brought to us in that big cardboard box, but there was no cardboard that would hold him now. We took him out of the large carrier. He was anxious to go; he screeched, but now it seemed that he knew this was his time. We would not stick him with any more needles, we would not force food down his throat, there were no more annoying drops to be squirted into his squinting, blinking eye. Not one more hour did he have to spend in our unwanted company.

One boost from our hands and the hawk was gone. He did not hesitate. He streaked up into the air, he flapped his strong, full wings, and wasted no time in reclaiming his place in the sky. The day was his; the autumn winds took him high and far out of our sight. There would be no gunshots today, no one waiting to brutally shoot him out of the air—only a few humans standing quietly in awe of his magnificent will, his undaunted spirit, and his miraculous recovery.

Perhaps this Earth will always be inhabited by people who care more about their "fun," more about material things, people who have souls that seem only half alive. But I choose to believe that the day will come when money is not more important than nature; when people look on a flower or tree or a hawk flying playfully in the sky and see a beauty that they know they are a part of, not separate from. Perhaps living in this time is like living through a drought—every day you know you must be one day closer to a wonderful rain shower. And as we have seen, the rain showers do indeed come.